the Joy of Writing Things Down

the Joy of Writing Things Down

THE EVERYDAY ZEN OF PUTTING PEN TO PAPER

Megan C. Hayes

greenfinch

First published in Great Britain in 2021 by
Greenfinch
An imprint of Quercus Editions Ltd
Carmelite House
50 Victoria Embankment
London EC4Y 0DZ

An Hachette UK company

A CIP catalogue record for this book is available from the
British Library

HB ISBN 978-1-52941-299-4
eBook ISBN 978-1-52941-300-7

10 9 8 7 6 5 4 3 2

Design by Tokiko Morishima
Cover and interior artwork by Romy Palstra

Printed in Italy

Papers used by Greenfinch are from well-managed forests and other
responsible sources.

Contents

Introduction 6

CHAPTER 1: **Lists** 28
Lists You're Already Writing 32
Lists to Try 49

CHAPTER 2: **Correspondence** 62
Correspondence You're Already Writing 67
Correspondence to Try 86

CHAPTER 3: **Notes to Self** 98
Notes You're Already Writing 103
Notes to Try 118

CHAPTER 4: **Journals and Diaries** 130
Journal and Diary Writing You're Already Doing 134
Journal and Diary Writing to Try 148

CHAPTER 5: **Goals and Plans** 164
Goals and Plans You're Already Writing 169
Goals and Plans to Try 184

AFTERWORD: **The Pleasure of Writing** 196

Endnotes 200
Further Reading 204
Index 205
Acknowledgements 208

Introduction

Humans have long organized our lives by putting pen to paper. We understand ourselves best, it seems, when we see what we're about reflected in type, whether on the physical page or digital screen. The problem we face in the modern day is that writing – something that has traditionally been a meditative, quiet and focused activity – has become just another rushed endeavour in the flurry of our lives.

We fire off 'instant' messages, 'shoot' emails at one another, jot down notes under pressure, pen harried shopping lists and scribble brief notes to self all while barely giving these tasks a second thought. This book encourages you to change that. This book is an invitation to make your writing habits a little more attentive, helpful and positive. In short, each chapter is designed to offer you a new, slightly more celebratory yet still highly pragmatic approach to writing things down.

How to Enjoy This Book

The following sections tie together a plethora of commonplace writing habits into one handy compendium. Every chapter begins with a little bit of background philosophy on a particular habit, from daily lists all the way through to bigger life goals and plans. You will then be invited to explore how that writing practice may currently play a role in your life – whether that's lengthy social media posts, work emails or to-do lists – and, hopefully, develop some new twists on these old favourites. You will also be introduced to a few wholly new versions of that habit, which you are not as likely to be practising. These are designed to offer fun, mindful and creative new ways to put words down on paper.

You can read the book cover to cover, or dip in and out of chapters that might hold particular interest. To truly get the most from these practical chapters, however, you will probably want to begin by getting familiar with the joyful philosophy of writing that underpins the book, which is set out on pages 11–27. From writing lists and correspondence, to more personal forms of writing like notes to self, journals and goals, the following chapters are peppered with more mindful ways to *practise* writing. Yet any practice – to be truly meaningful in our lives – is usually underpinned by a helpful theory, or philosophy: the 'why' to the 'how'. This book guides you towards a more joyful philosophy of writing.

Uncover Your Creativity

Writing is a highly personal and creative practice. For writing to form a truly joyful habit in your life, it is critical to approach this in a way that allows for your own individual creative flair. This is because forging habits that are imbued with autonomy and self-direction, i.e. tailored to *us*, makes these habits a lot more likely to stick.

You are invited, with every single prompt and activity in this book, to adapt and recreate the suggested tips in whatever ways might make them most meaningful and beneficial for *you*. Swap out a word or point of focus for something else? Sure. Reorder the steps of a given exercise? Go for it. This book and the ideas it contains are only significant in application, and you are the one that gets to do the applying – so do it in a way that works for you, however novel or creative.

While we don't tend to think of shopping lists, or notes to self or everyday emails as creative activities – they are. We might think of 'creative writing' as synonymous with wildly imaginative or fictional writing. Yet this can limit our other, more personal, forms of writing to a model that is really rather dry. We scoff that we 'just aren't creative people' and therefore deny ourselves the joy of *everyday* creativity. The truth is that *all* kinds of writing are, to a greater or lesser degree, creative, because they involve ingenuity – albeit day-to-day ingenuity that we might currently take for granted (a bit like being able to bake some bread, or organize a shelf beautifully).

Indeed, the experience of being human is an inherently creative experience. There is one school of thought in psychology that holds that we construct our very lives creatively; we come to understand the world based on patterns in our past experience and use these, along with a dash of imagination, to construe what is likely to happen to us next.[1] Sometimes these constructions are helpful and guide us in beneficial ways, but at other times these ideas about our lives can be very unhelpful, i.e. limiting or short-sighted. This is one reason why writing is such a useful practice, because it allows us to unravel and examine these constructions in greater detail.

Your Existing Philosophy of Writing Things Down

Before reading further, you might like to take a moment to consider what your current construction, theory or philosophy of writing is and involves. Is this habit purely practical for you, or do you pen the odd poem? Do you write in regimented ways, or allow your mind to wander spontaneously? Do you revere the 'freewriting'[2] technique (keeping your hand moving without worrying about grammar, spelling or structure), or do you perhaps prefer to be more reflective and expressive, delving deep to find the perfect way to express a certain idea or sentiment? Are you a grammar nerd, or more inclined towards 'automatic' writing (producing words, real or made up, without consciously thinking about what you are writing)?

These questions are important to ask as you begin your journey towards a more focused and fulfilling writing practice; if we know how we *already* approach this habit, then we can get a clearer idea of where we might like to journey next. If you keep a journal, take some time now to write about why, and how, you currently use writing. You will then have this information to hand as you explore the following chapters; this will act as a helpful touchstone against which you can assess the new habits that might best fit you, or push you a little way out of your comfort zone.

Finally, whatever surprising philosophical insights, practical prompts or beneficial tips you may take from these pages, remember to approach writing in a spirit of light-

heartedness and experimentation. Choose not to get bogged down in any 'shoulds', 'proper' approaches or 'must dos'; simply let writing be what you need it to be (that's when it tends to work best for us, after all).

A More Joyful Philosophy of Writing Things Down

There is no 'right' way to write. If there were, writing would be a truly monotonous affair. Writing things down is useful to humans precisely *because* it is so singular to each of us: it is our thoughts that we are penning, after all. As such, the philosophy of writing set out here is not intended to be didactic or by any means the final word on how one must put pen to paper. The way this habit plays out in your own life will always be a subjective matter.

What the following philosophy *does* offer is a fresh new way to look at a long-beloved process, providing a few guiding principles (should you wish to adopt them). Use the ideas set out in the following pages simply as prompts to begin asking questions of your own writing habits, namely:

- Where and in what ways might I direct more of my *attention* to my writing habits?
- Where and in what ways might my writing habits become increasingly *helpful* to me?
- Where and in what ways might I gain greater *positive benefit* from my writing habits?

Make Your Writing Habits More Attentive

If humans have a superpower, it is our attention. Yet this power is not always easy to wield. In the modern day, we regularly fall victim to attention-leeching black holes: phones, screens, adverts, incoming messages, apps and the Internet at large. Historically, we have also long fallen victim to other perennial attention-thieves: worry, toil, other people's expectations and suffering more generally. Thus, many traditions around the world have evolved to teach techniques that help us manage our attention, offering guidance in directing it in more helpful and productive directions.

Two of these traditional approaches to attentiveness that are particularly pertinent to the practice of writing things down, and from which this book draws, are the theory and practice of psychology (developed in the West in the 19th century) and the more spiritual practice of Zen Buddhism (developed in the East some 2,500 years ago).

What do these, on the surface of things, really rather divergent human practices have in common? Well, both can be called 'uncovering' practices, each designed to unearth insights into our deepest nature, thoughts and feelings.[3] These two traditions reveal a more meaningful philosophy of writing things down, because writing, too, is a kind of uncovering practice. Let's explore this a little further.

THE EVERYDAY THERAPEUTIC EFFECTS OF WRITING

Most of us are familiar with the idea of the psyche – the human mind, soul or spirit that resides within each of us as a cluster of thoughts, feelings and emotions. Classic and contemporary psychology alike have much to teach us about the workings of this inner self. Such theory is often applied in a practice we call psychotherapy, or 'talk therapy', in which we might gradually share and shape a narrative about our experiences, hopes and dreams with a professional. The psychotherapeutic approach, then, is one that asks us to pause and look at our lives reflectively and compassionately with another. Yet, while not all of us will seek formal therapy of this kind, we can all stand to benefit from greater understanding of our individual psyche – or *attentiveness to our own inner world*. We can be helped in this aim by writing things down.

Many hundreds of scientific studies have now accounted for the therapeutic effects of writing about our thoughts and feelings, predominantly led by contemporary researcher James W Pennebaker, Professor of Psychology at the University of Texas at Austin, USA. These effects include measurable boosts to both emotional wellbeing and, in some cases, even physical wellbeing. More anecdotally, writers and philosophers have for many centuries extolled the benefits of putting our thoughts into words as a way to gain greater self-understanding, calmness and happiness.

Currently, there is no one, reigning scientific theory that succinctly captures why writing things down can often be so helpful for us. Might we hypothesize that writing is, simply, a way of 'storying' our experience – of bringing our thoughts and feelings *to our own attention*, so that we can understand our selves a little better? If so, let us now turn to a far longer-standing tradition of bringing our selves to our own attention.

THE EVERYDAY ZEN OF WRITING

Zen is a Japanese concept that literally means 'meditation', yet it originates in the Chinese *chán*, meaning 'quietude'.[4] It describes a particular school of Buddhist thought and practice that involves seated meditation, usually under the guidance of a teacher, with the intention of reaching enlightenment. In contemporary terms, the aim of meditation of this kind is to bring one's awareness to the present moment *just as it is* in order to promote calm and wellbeing.

Writing more attentively, in the spirit of everyday Zen, or quietude, isn't necessarily about carving out more time that you don't have or spending hours in meditation. It is about revelling in the untapped source of reflective peace and quiet to be found in a regular habit: writing. It is a way of, simply, *living what you are living*. Writing with everyday Zen attentiveness is a manner of existing in the moment of your life that is happening right now. If you are sweeping, sweep. If you are sipping tea, sip tea. If you are writing, write.

This sounds simple enough, yet many of us are plagued by the affliction of *not* living what we are living. We live, instead, a little bit in yesterday; there was that daft thing we said in a work meeting, or that bill we really should have sorted, or that person we were meant to call back. We also live a little bit in tomorrow; there is that tough topic of conversation we need to bring up with a colleague, and that visit next week from our parents, as well as that important goal we really should have got around to completing by now. As compelling as it sounds, the well-worn maxim to 'live in the moment' is not something we are very good, in practice, at upholding.

Putting pen to paper, or our fingers to our keypads, is one practice where we can learn to exist more mindfully and in the spirit of everyday Zen. This is because writing features frequently in most of our lives, offering an opportunity to focus closely on the task at hand (thus naturally providing a quiet or meditative moment). Yet you might currently write things down several times a day without thinking much about this at all. Precisely because this task can at times be a bit of a mind-*less* one, it is the perfect place to begin a practice of mind-*ful* everyday Zen. By bringing our attention to the very ordinary tasks in our lives, we can cultivate the ability to live with ever more focused awareness – becoming (one hopes) increasingly mindful, conscious and 'awake' in all that we do.

Make Your Writing Habits More Helpful

Many, if not most, of us experience the thoughts in our head as a kind of narrator speaking to us. Sometimes, we experience multiple narrators; there is the voice of a stern parent, kind friend or an old schoolteacher...voices we've embodied over the years and that all serve to give us varying kinds of useful (and, often, not so useful) advice. This can become confusing, rather noisy and a little crowded.

Experiencing these 'voices' is not a sign that we are losing the thread of reality or becoming dangerously fragmented – not at all. Researchers have long demonstrated that this happens because we tend to think in language (rather than visually), and language is social – we inherit it from other people (think of a toddler learning to talk with their parents). We can think of the self, then, not as one single voice, but more like a dialogue or discourse.[5] Our thoughts are a kind of inner speech, and writing things down, therefore, is a way of this inner speech becoming externalized.[6]

This externalized inner speech can serve many functions; writing is an organizing tool, a communication tool and even a self-soothing tool. Writing things down is, if you like, a way of developing a *helping relationship* with one's thoughts, and with one's self. The humanistic psychologist, Carl Rogers, pioneered a theory of what makes for a good helping relationship between two people (such as a therapist and client, or teacher and student). The theory is based on three core conditions that when met, Rogers theorized, would help liberate the student or client to express their truest thoughts and feelings in such a way that they felt free from the fear of judgement.[7]

It turns out these conditions are also rather helpful when thinking about writing things down. Only, in this case, these conditions help us to forge a more helpful relationship *with ourselves*. They are: congruence, unconditional positive regard and empathic understanding.

WRITE MORE CONGRUENTLY
(i.e. in a way that is aligned with your true feelings)

We can often feel a strange sense of being somewhat divorced from ourselves. We aren't always sure of what we feel; or, perhaps, we *are* sure but are actively choosing to suppress or ignore difficult feelings. This is the opposite of congruence.

Writing or saying positive affirmations, setting lofty goals or writing overly ambitious to-do lists – if these are not things that we truly feel or believe ourselves capable of at a core level – might be, unsurprisingly, really quite damaging. Remaining aware of the level of congruence in our writing (i.e. how closely what we are putting on paper actually matches up with what we feel to be true) is paramount to writing becoming a helpful habit in our lives.

To begin approaching your writing habits more congruently, ask yourself: does this feel true? Am I being genuine?

Is there another, deeper truth? Does what I've written reflect the 'real me'?

Other ways to think about congruence are: realness, transparency, genuineness or authenticity.

WRITE WITH UNCONDITIONAL POSITIVE REGARD
(i.e. accept without judgement)

When you write, how do you 'receive' your own words? Do you sometimes (secretly or not so secretly) observe your notes and emails and diary entries as the desperate scribbles of a woefully unproductive good-for-nothing? Or, perhaps, is there a low-level sense of dissatisfaction at the un-met goals piling up on your to-do list?

While a healthy dose of self-awareness and self-critique is paramount to accurate self-knowledge and accountability, if this verges on *non-acceptance* of the self then we might begin to experience a very uncomfortable inner relationship. When it comes to writing, perhaps the best way to understand this is not in the sense of writing down 'I'm great at everything and there are no flies on me', but instead developing the ability to write 'I could possibly improve on a great many things about myself' and, simply, *accepting* that fact without judgement. To acknowledge both the light and dark within oneself is a great, and really rather mature, skill to develop (though not always easy).

To begin approaching your writing habits with greater positive regard, ask yourself: how might I accept, and even

Other ways to think about unconditional positive regard are: caring, prizing, warm acceptance of, and interest in, what's going on within our selves.

embrace, my very human fallibility? What would be different if I were to see my efforts as 'enough'? Which things about me are really not so perfect, and how might I become comfortable with these parts?

WRITE WITH EMPATHIC UNDERSTANDING (i.e. acknowledging the self accurately and kindly)

Developing empathy in our writing takes us one step further than the level of positive regard, to write in such a way that we *understand and respond to ourselves kindly*. Recall what we said earlier about our inner world being rather more of a dialogue than a monologue. What is the tone of that conversation, in your own mind (or on the page)? Are you intrigued to know more when emotions arise within you, or do you dismiss some parts of your self and experience?

We are often, and with acerbic consistency, our own harshest critics. If a friend or loved one has ever told you not to be so tough on yourself, or if you have noticed a train of inner dialogue that was just plain mean, then you might benefit from approaching your writing habits with a little more empathy.

Interestingly, one group of researchers led by Yi Cheng Lin at National Taiwan University found that writing in the second person, i.e. stating '*you* felt xyz' rather than '*I* felt xyz', might help us to relate more kindly to ourselves in the spirit of greater self-support.[8] Whether it is a simple daily to-do list, or more personal writing in a journal, writing things down as a literal dialogue between 'you' and 'I' is one way we can write with greater empathy. Again, this is not a case of the blind optimism of 'you are great at everything' but a bit more like 'I noticed you tried really hard today in the following ways'.

To begin approaching your writing habits with greater empathic understanding, ask yourself: how might I listen to myself with greater kindness? Do I fully understand the meaning of this experience? Can I reach a deeper sense of significance, or understanding of this aspect of myself?

Other ways to think about empathic understanding are: really listening, inquisitiveness, curiosity and awareness of personal meaning.

Make Your Writing Habits More Joyful

Writing things down has long been heralded as cathartic. We tend to have a shared understanding, or philosophy, of writing as something that helps us organize our unwieldy or difficult thoughts and get things off of our chest.

Contemporary psychology has continued in this trend, evidencing how expressing our fears, pain and shame on paper makes us feel both emotionally and physically better. This is an interesting yet highly *deficit-orientated* understanding of what writing is and what it does for us. In the real world – i.e. out of the science lab and into the wilds of modern life – there are many positive and joyful benefits of writing regularly (these are, incidentally, now also being increasingly studied by the lab-dwellers). Writing is a form of self-affirmation, a way to pinpoint our deepest values, broaden our perspective, and it is, simply, enjoyable.[9] Is it necessary, then, to update our philosophy of writing to something a little more positive? This book argues that, yes, it is.

Yet – does the word 'positive' sometimes make you feel a bit distrustful? Perturbed, even? You are not alone. In a world where things are often complex, challenging and at times just pretty awful, many people sense that it is twee, glib or even dangerously naïve to buy into the idea of a positive philosophy of, well, anything. Yet this begs the question: what do we actually mean when we talk about positivity?

We can understand positivity as a deeply complex and nuanced human experience. Most of us are familiar with the concept of *yin-yang* from Eastern philosophy. This concept captures, in a most simplistic sense, the manner in which opposing forces can coexist in interconnected harmony. Positivity and ostensible 'negativity' may also be viewed this way.

To understand the significance of this you might reflect on the fact that, were one not to have ever had any negative experiences – i.e. painful or sad or not-very-pleasurable kinds of experiences – then how might that person know what a positive experience *was*? They wouldn't, because that person would have no way of distinguishing it from

any *opposing* kind of experience. This is to say that we can only helpfully discuss positivity with a shared understanding of what 'not positive' is and feels like. Unhappiness does, in a very profound manner, teach us what happiness is – just as the opposite is also true.

I'm sure you can recall for yourself what your 'not positive' experiences have been like. You might, possibly, want to have fewer of these experiences. If you find yourself *disagreeing* with this (i.e. 'my negative experiences were valuable!') then you might explore if, actually, the experiences about which you've been thinking actually were, oddly, positive in their own way – in other words that they were meaningful or self-defining or excellent learning opportunities. All rather positive things, you might say. Thus, the symbiotic, interlaced nature of these two becomes starkly evident.

So, in approaching our writing more positively, or joyfully, we give ourselves the opportunity to name (and witness) the *totality* of our experience on the page: the good and the not-so-good. Indeed, we begin to see ourselves as in flux between these so-called poles – we become, as Carl Rogers remarked, content with ourselves as a *process* rather than final *product*.[10] Nevertheless, we also grant ourselves the chance to *construe* that process as one in which we are moving towards growth, greater wellbeing and happiness.

When we write, we pen our own kind of story about things. Making that story an ultimately joyful one is a choice we get to make whenever our pen meets the page.

Bringing It All Together

These three tenets of a more joyful philosophy of writing – as an attentive, helpful and positive practice – demonstrate the many varied ways in which writing is an opportunity to *more clearly experience what we are experiencing*. Writing grants us greater access to our thoughts, hopes, ambitions, ideas and our plans.

While many writing tasks provide the opportunity to apply all three of these 'ways of experiencing' simultaneously, you might find it useful to view the philosophy set out here as more of a toolbox of approaches from which you can gather inspiration as needed.

Take a moment now to review these three ways of understanding writing and to ask: which most interests you right now? Which feels like something you already practise in your note-taking, correspondence, journal or other writing habits? Where might you have the opportunity to grow and develop?

1. Writing can help you bring attention to your thoughts or to the present moment.
2. Writing can foster a supportive internal dialogue that feels authentic, non-judgemental and empathetic.
3. Writing can capture the totality of your experiences, both the good and the bad, in a way that supports self-development and growth.

The Rewards of Writing

It is perhaps worth remembering that, while writing things down can be a commonplace, perhaps even humdrum activity, it also has its own certain kind of magic. When we put things down on paper we open up a world of possibility. That white sheet of A4 is a realm of potential. The notebook is a territory of invention. The sticky note is a space of wonders yet to be.

Is this why the blank page can, at times, be a little terrifying? Whether we want to begin a novel or write a heartfelt letter, we sometimes find we are paralysed before we have even started; we avoid beginning lest we begin in the 'wrong' way (i.e. make fools of ourselves somehow). Yes – writing involves risk, but let this new philosophy guide you as you begin a deeper kind of adventure with writing. Let it be a reminder that, as with many risks we take in life, the *rewards* we experience when we put words on paper can be great.

General Tips for Mindful Writing

Joy is a physical as well as an emotional experience (we jump for joy, smile with joy and experience joyful anticipation as 'butterflies' in our tummies). What is more is that, because the writing habit is so common in our daily lives, it can serve as a useful chance to check in with how we feel somatically, i.e. in our bodies and not just our minds.

Researchers increasingly demonstrate the deeply intertwined ways in which mind and body work together as one system; calming thoughts can produce physiological calm and vice versa. Use the following tips – whenever you catch yourself writing a note or shooting off an email – to write with your body and not just your mind.

As we move through this book, return to these general tips. By attaching them to your regular writing activities you will soon find a whole new realm of calm hiding in your day – pockets of Zen quietude in your life, just as it is.

- Use the writing task as an opportunity to take a few deep breaths, release your tongue from the roof your mouth and relax your jaw and shoulders (if you are holding any tension there).

- Notice your feet resting on the ground and the steadiness of the chair or surface beneath you. Rest more deeply against this steadiness. Bring your attention to the feeling of being held and supported by this surface.

- Become closely aware of the physical space around you: the width of the room, the landscape beyond and the height of the sky above you. Breathe in from that expansive space, and out into it.

- Become closely aware of the activity: what does the pen feel like in your hand? How do the keys of your laptop sound beneath the drum of your fingers? Notice these sensations without judgement – just let them be there.

- Become aware of your physical body and any sensations you might be feeling – again without judgment. Simply notice the feeling and let it be there. If writing with a pen, you may like to place your free hand on your tummy – the place where we describe having 'gut' feelings, where we feel nervous and where we sense our excitement – and notice what, if anything, you are feeling there.

- Settle yourself into the moment. Choose not to think about what you were doing five minutes ago, or your worries for tomorrow. Attend to this precise moment fully and completely.

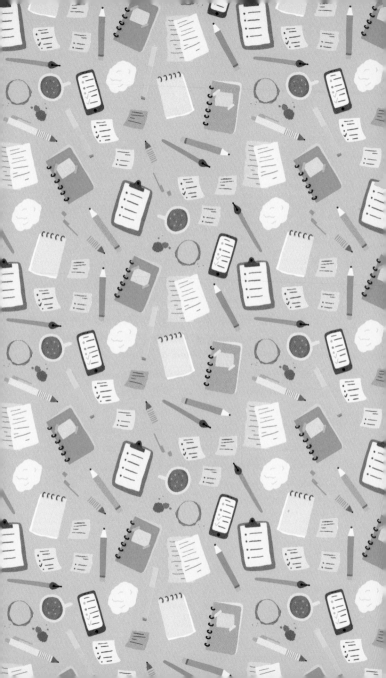

Lists

From shopping lists and to-do lists to cataloguing ideas and information inventories – there are few things quite as satisfying as an orderly column of information that we want to remember. The act of writing a list can instantly quell anxiety and help us to feel we have a handle on a muddle of material or accumulation of tasks. In this chapter, let your use of lists reach new heights as you focus in on what makes your day-to-day meaningful and magical – and put that most important of information into your list-writing rituals.

Writing of all kinds empowers us to, we might say, *talk about our thoughts*. Nowhere is this more evident than in our list writing. The philosophy behind the list is to make sense of what we think and to give us a feeling of control over our external world. The act of creating a list offers a scaffold to hold otherwise disordered parts together. We perform a kind of alchemy when we compose lists, constructing pattern from disorder. Thus we have long used lists for *organization*. Consider our calendars, genealogies and even our dictionaries. All of these have helped us manage information – and our lives. The list form, it seems, has been at the very heart of human civilizations for centuries.[1]

Looked at this way, the list is a small miracle. Yet it is important to note that this human fixation with orderliness – of which the humble list is an emblem – is something of an illusion. Our universe is better defined by an opposing philosophy: something known as *entropy*, or the gradual decline into disorderliness. The gathering together of *stuff* into the form of a list is, in fact, an endearingly naïve – and very human – activity in a beautiful but chaotic world. Other mammals don't inventory their needs and wants. Fish don't compose bucket lists. Birds don't bullet point agendas for meetings. These other species are far less attached to orderliness – and, sometimes, it is our human need to organize and order that can lead to increased anxiety and stress.

Perhaps you are already in a list-writing habit. Perhaps your home is scattered with reporter's pads and notebooks and magnetic-backed pads stuck on the fridge. We keep lists for a reason: to help us remember the *stuff* of our lives, whether that be mounting administrative tasks, or things we need for the food cupboard. Yet what if lists could do more for us than simply provide a holder for this humdrum information? What if we used the list-writing habit to help us recall what's *most* important to us, too? If our lists also kept track of the things we *really* want to remember, such as who and what we love, why we're grateful to be here at all and what it is that makes our lives worth living?

The exercises in this chapter will help you bring a fresh and playful spirit to your list writing – transforming this practice into so much more than an organizational tool.

Lists
You're
Already
Writing

You may never have given much thought to why you write lists; it seems somehow *instinctual* that we would manage and record the daily goings on of a life with pen and paper. Yet it is precisely such habits that can benefit from a more mindful approach. This little secular ritual can be as poignant as we make up our minds for it to be. So much of our *being* human is about the things we are *doing*. And, yes, it might be helpful to shut off from all that busy human doing by taking a yoga class or meditating or walking a mountain trail – but does that mean our day-to-day rituals are left to be frenetic and frenzied? Of course not. We can approach our *doing* behaviours with just the same spirit of sacredness.

Perhaps the best place to begin a more mindful and meaningful list-writing habit is by looking to where lists already exist in your life. Where does this ritual currently feature in your day? Is your coffee table awash with bulleted notes on home decoration projects? Are there colourful Post-its adorning your work computer like petals on a strange-looking plant? Excellent. Start there. Use the exercises in this chapter to reconceptualize this habit you already have.

As you try out these new twists on an established habit, remember to *approach lists with playfulness*. Next time you find yourself fashioning a list that you imagine to be sacred in its certainty and specificity – stop to have a kindly chuckle at yourself. As you write, remind yourself of this: we do not have complete control of our lives. Ironically, it is thinking that we *do* or *should* have control of these events that is the source of much of our frustration.

Avoid attempts to steer the river of your experience in your list writing. While you can always organize information into orderly patterns, the world is wide and shapeshifting. In truth, you might often have very little influence over what happens to you – in your day, in a given project, etc. Let this bring you peace rather than perturb you. The list is an enjoyable – maybe very necessary – exercise, but it doesn't give us absolute control. That's okay – absolute control would be a lot more responsibility than we would really want to carry, wouldn't it?

The To-do List

Whether you have yours scribed decoratively in chalk on a blackboard wall in your kitchen, or scrambled together in the Notes app on your phone, it is likely you have some kind of to-do list habit. And that's a good thing, because research has shown that writing down what we intend to get done makes us more likely to achieve it.[2] Here are some tips to get more everyday mindful benefit from that most commonplace of writing practices: the to-do list.

TRY SHARING YOUR TO-DO LIST

If your to-do list practice is currently working well for you, then by all means forge on. If, however, you find your lists rarely get checked off – it might be worth taking a different approach. One helpful way of doing this is to share your list with somebody else. You might exchange

lists with a good friend at the start of each week to keep each other accountable. Or you might make your to-do list entirely collaborative by planning to complete important tasks in tandem, such as syncing your grocery shop with a friend you already meet for a coffee morning, or by bringing a team together for a work project rather than trying to get it done alone (there are many apps and online tools that can assist in sharing your 'to dos', such as Trello or Quip). A to-do list shared can be a to-do list halved.

TRY WRITING YOUR TO-DO LIST AT BEDTIME

To-do lists might feel like a post-coffee, morning time sort of practice, but did you know that bedtime might be the best moment to reap the benefits of this habit – and that switching things up this way might even help you sleep? Common sense would suggest bedtime as a moment to recount the events of the day just passed, as we might in a personal journal, but one group of researchers recently found that writing about what we have *done* on a given day might actually negatively affect sleep versus writing about what we want to *get done* on the next.[3] The study suggested that taking five minutes before bed to plan what you anticipate doing the next day, or in the coming days, might actually help you drop off quicker. Intuitively, this actually makes a lot of sense. List writing involves offloading any potential tasks onto the page where we know we won't forget them, allowing us to subsequently relax and drift off. Give it a go yourself and see.

TRY CATEGORIZING YOUR TO-DO LIST

It is common for our to-do lists to become repositories for the most mundane of tasks. Dominated by administrative duties and household chores, we might begin to find this habit really rather dry. A potential antidote is to compartmentalize the items on your to-do list into different categories. This will serve not only to diversify your activities day to day ('all work and no play' becoming, hopefully, a thing of the past), but it will also serve as a helpful thermometer indicating the areas of your life you are neglecting to nourish.

It is likely that these categories will be very personal, but a good starting point might be the work of Carol Ryff, Professor of Psychology at the University of Wisconsin-Madison in the USA, whose research has asked: *what are the essential features of wellbeing?*[4] Building on decades of research by thought leaders including Carl Jung, Carl Rogers and Marie Jahoda, Ryff and her colleagues have identified six building blocks of feeling well. Try crafting your to-do list with at least one task tailored under each heading as shown in the examples opposite.

SELF-ACCEPTANCE
* 20 minutes of exercise to feel good in my body.
* Say the affirmation 'I am enough' in my morning shower.

PURPOSE
* 20 minutes on a meaningful project such as writing my novel.
* Clean the kitchen as an act of self-care.

POSITIVE RELATIONSHIPS
* 20-minute phone call with Mum where I listen closely and focus.
* Thank a colleague sincerely for their help.

PERSONAL GROWTH
* 20 minutes reflective journal writing.
* Try learning a new dance step via YouTube.

POSITIVE RELATIONSHIP WITH ENVIRONMENT
* 20 minutes clearing desk of clutter.
* Work an hour per day outside.

AUTONOMY
* 20 minutes on an independent project at work.
* Set a boundary by telling friends I'll be offline this weekend.

The Bucket List

The bigger sibling of the to-do list is the bucket list. What, this list asks, will we do, not only with our days and weeks, but with our *lives*? You would think that such a list might be the most sacred of them all, and yet many of us either haven't written these down physically at all, or else maybe did once but couldn't for the life of us tell you where it is. Nevertheless, for a great many of us, some version of this lists exists, even if it is just in the backs of our minds.

Your bucket list might be very traditional and straightforward: travel, succeed in chosen career, marry, have kids, be happy. Or perhaps it is awash with white-knuckle solo adventures and spiritual experiences you are sure you'll have time for someday. Below is one new way to look at this old habit.

WRITE THE STORY OF YOUR 'BEST-POSSIBLE SELF'

Researchers have put their own spin on the classic bucket list by re-envisaging it as more of a narrative, or story. In psychology this is known as the 'Best-possible Self' exercise.[5] The original study asked participants to write about a positive future self, for whom everything had gone as well as possible, for 20 minutes per day over four consecutive days. The results suggested a significant increase in subjective wellbeing, i.e. a positive sense about one's quality of life.

While a more recent study has evidenced the importance of setting *realistic* expectations (to avoid a life of perpetual disappointment),[6] your bucket list might nevertheless be reinvigorated by the following twist:

1. Think about what your life might look like in the future, imagining all has gone as well as possible; all your major goals are accomplished and your dreams have all been realized.

2. Next, write for 20 minutes about what you imagined. Use as much description as you like, putting yourself in the shoes of that potential future self.

3. A common regret of people at the end of their lives is not having had the bravery to forge their own path. As you imagine your best-possible self, ask yourself how true this is to your deeper nature: are the things you are imagining realistic and authentic goals? Do you *really* want these things?

4. Notice anything surprising in this 'story'. Who do you hope is still there in the future with you? What will likely be most important once all your career, financial or travel goals are complete? What will that ideal life feel like – restful, joyous, bold, fulfilled?

5. Next, write out your bucket list afresh. Has anything changed? What seems more, or less, important after having written this story of your future self?

Imagining a 'best-possible' scenario is certainly not the *only* way one should write about one's life (a healthy dose of defensive pessimism and sense of surrender to the current of things are also advised). Nevertheless, this may be a helpful exercise to visualize exactly what those dreams you imagine you are ticking off might mean for your life once achieved.

The Address or Birthday List

Do you keep an address book to log your friends and family's whereabouts? Or a birthday book to help you remember who needs a card when? This kind of list is a typical habit for many of us. Keeping track of the significant data associated with those we love, or with whom we are merely acquainted, is a truly endearing human behaviour. It is heart-warming that, despite our proclivity for discord, disagreements and conflict, we truly do desire to be close to one another. The simple act of sending a card on a meaningful date is evidence of this.

What is more is that it isn't just *nice* to have a log of people we love, like or perhaps once lived alongside – it is actually a major (if not *the* major) resource in a fulfilling, contented life. One way that psychologists describe this shared sense of identity through empathic interpersonal connections is *social capital*. Thus, when you wish a colleague good luck in their new home, or send birthday wishes to your niece, you are quite literally making an investment in your own wellbeing. Positive social connections bolster our health like deposits at the bank bolster wealth.

With this knowledge, whether you log your addresses digitally or in a dedicated and beautifully bound book, this is a habit you can infuse with a little more meaning. As you meet or connect with a new person and add their information to your address book or birthday book, why not try adding one or more of the following additional titbits to help you focus on your own web of social wealth?

Write a short statement of something you admire about the person. Are they admirably forthright? Are they a pillar of the community? Fantastic tennis player? Make a note of this beside their name, e.g. 'Sara (scintillating political debater)'.

Write something specific you are grateful for in that person. Did they once do something exceptionally kind, or perhaps regularly offer you support and guidance in some way? Make a note beside their name to remind you what this connection means to you, even if it is something seemingly small.

Write a specific way in which you know you can count on that person. They might provide a listening ear when you need it, give great restaurant recommendations or even offer practical support whenever you run into hardship.

The Shopping List

If there was ever a list that was almost as ubiquitous as the list-writing habit itself, it's the shopping list. What is it about that tube of toothpaste or bunch of bananas that makes them so easy to forget (unless we commit them to paper)? Who knows, but next time you scribble out your dearth of bread and teabags – why not enrich your shopping list with one or more of the following? Yes, even this tiny unexciting errand can become a source of wellbeing with a simple tweak or two.

Treat your shopping list as a gratitude practice. As you write each of your groceries down, say a quiet internal word of thanks that you are able to afford it and will enjoy cooking and eating it with family or friends. To extend this, you may also like to add three *additional* things you're grateful for to your shopping list, such as pleasant weather, time spent with a friend, a great book you are reading, or anything at all that has been bolstering you and bringing you joy – however small.

Shop a little; give a little. Living in the spirit of service to others is something of a radical act when we live in highly individualistic environments. Yet the sense of being bound to others in helping, reciprocal 'gift economies' is an ancient human habit that traverses almost all cultures at all historical moments; we depend upon one another in ways that, in modern existence, it can be easy to forget.[7] Once per month, perhaps you might tally up the cost of your weekly shopping list and donate that same amount to a local food bank. If you aren't in the financial position to do this, why not offer to collect some groceries for an elderly neighbour instead. As if by magic, your weekly shopping list will become a profound and soulful reminder of your interconnectedness with others.

Add an affirmation. Picking up your weekly groceries on the rush home from work before hotfooting to the gym or cooking and clearing up the family meal often leaves little time to pause and reflect. To counter this, write an affirmation at the top of the notepad where you keep your shopping list; something along the lines of 'I have access to all I need and I am safe'. Each time you go to add an item to your list, take a deep breath and state the affirmation out loud or internally, allowing your shoulders to drop and unwind.

The Project List

Even the grandest of projects – be that a work venture or personal passion project like starting a vegetable garden from scratch – will often begin in the most humble of forms: the hastily jotted list. We write down an email address, someone we want to ask something, some things we need to purchase or a few step-by-step actions we need to take...Sure, we will flesh out the details later, but the inception of a project regularly begins as a bare-bones list.

At the heart of any project is one very endearing human emotion: hope. We wouldn't be likely to invest much time or effort in a complex venture unless we felt that, when it came down to it, we were likely to fulfil our aims. Research has proven that higher levels of hope are consistent with better outcomes in situations as wide-ranging as athletics, physical health and even psychotherapy.[8] Simply put, then, if we want our project-planning lists to work harder for us and yield better outcomes, we would be wise to infuse them with a little more hope.

TRY THIS

Next time you are beginning to plan a project using a list, take a moment to think closely about how hopeful you are about seeing the project through to fruition. According to hope theory, there are two principal ways in which we think in a hopeful way about achieving our goals; these are known as 'pathway thoughts' and 'agency thoughts'. Pathway thoughts involve the specific route or set of steps required to complete a goal, while agency thoughts involve our sense of motivation and ability to direct our energy toward the task.

Most of our planning lists would probably come under *pathway* thinking, with little thought given to our sense of *agency* (or motivation). Therefore, make your list more hopeful by splitting it under two subheadings, 'PATH' and 'MOTIVATION'. For every step under PATH, e.g. 'buy compost at the garden centre', add a note under

MOTIVATION about how and when you will manifest this step, e.g. 'Saturday morning is when I'll have the most energy for the trip'.

PATH	MOTIVATION
Buy compost at the garden centre	Saturday morning is when I'll have the most energy for the trip
Finish draft of novel	Wake up half an hour earlier than rest of household each day to avoid interruptions and ensure my mind is sharp
Knit a jumper for nephew	Try a virtual knitting circle with friends — we could work together via video call for accountability

Writing for Focus

Writing is a powerful way to achieve greater presence and awareness of the day-to-day goings on of a life. When we write a list in particular, we narrow the aperture of our awareness to a limited range of information – and this is what makes it such a helpful habit. This kind of writing can feel infinitely calming, because such a vast amount of modern life is spent scrolling, seeking, striving and – let's face it – feeling like we are sinking under infinite stimuli. Another word for focus is mindfulness and the benefits of this kind of awareness are significant: it can help us regulate our feelings and emotions, clarify our values and make us more flexible in the face of life changes, among other benefits.[1]

Here are three alternative ways of writing for focus that you might want to try when feeling world-weary or overwhelmed. Each could take as little as five to ten minutes, if that's all you have. Setting a quick five-minute timer in the morning or over your lunch break is doable for most of us and you may be surprised at the benefits of even five minutes' focused writing per day. If you have more time, take longer.

Write About an Object

In his collection, *Odes to Common Things*, the poet Pablo Neruda compiled an endearing compendium of poems that celebrate the ordinary, humdrum and commonplace things of a life. In the collection there are verses espousing the virtues of everything from the moon to an onion. Choose your own common thing – a pen on your desk, a clementine in the fruit bowl, a shoe – and write about it. This doesn't have to take the formal structure of a poem. You might simply list the features of the object, but do try to focus closely on it. Perhaps imagine that you are brand new to this planet and this is your first encounter with such an object. The idea is to centre your attention closely in a way that you might not normally.

Write a 'Pen Portrait'

The pen portrait is a technique long used by creative writers but that, more than fodder for fiction, is a wonderfully mindful activity in its own right. The idea is to capture a person's portrait in a short paragraph. This might be someone you know, or an interesting-looking stranger, or maybe someone you remember from long ago – anyone at all. Try to capture all the key observable elements that make up this person. What is their hair like? What are they wearing? What colour are their eyes (be as precise as possible, e.g. the blue-green of a marble)? What mannerisms or interesting quirks do they have? Think of this activity as capturing the person as a photo would, only with words instead of pixels. The idea here is to become more interested in – i.e. focused upon – those around you.

Write Alongside Nature

Humans have long stoked their soft spot for nature through writing. The poet Wendell Berry's poem 'The Peace of Wild Things' is a particularly lovely example, if you are looking for some inspiration. Nature soothes and fortifies us. So, too, does writing about nature. Try penning the view from your window, or recount what you saw on a recent walk. You might also sit in the garden or get out to the coast specifically to write about what you find there. Think of the micro (a tiny ladybird on a blade of grass) to the macro elements (the vastness of the horizon beyond you).

Lists
to Try

If list writing has not been top of your agenda to date, or if you would like to benefit more from the daily art of list writing, the following pages are arranged together just for you. While in the previous pages you traversed some commonplace lists you are likely to be writing already, in this section you are presented with a brand new plethora of lists you might try.

While it might feel ever harder to squeeze space in our lives for activities that boost our wellbeing – a few minutes spent jotting words down on paper has to be one of the simplest tasks to do. You don't need an hour, or special clothing, or total silence, or any grand tools or equipment. Yet adding a new list-writing habit might pay dividends in terms of comforting you in moments of anxiety all the way to bolstering your productive moments.

All of the suggestions in this section focus on wellbeing, but some are more calming while some are a little more output-focused. Peruse at your leisure to find a new list-writing habit that might just bring you a little joy in only a few bullet points.

The Five Senses List

When we are feeling at our most anxious it is not
uncommon to lose our awareness of the five senses. In
fact, many of us live the majority of our days and weeks
in this state of low-level detachment from our immediate
sensory experience of the world.

A common grounding technique to combat this tendency,
and one that is often recommended for those who
struggle with acute anxiety, is a quick five-step
acknowledgement of the various senses. This also makes
for a great writing exercise and can be profoundly calming.
While it is helpful when anxiety is acute, it is also a lovely
way to bring our awareness into the present moment at
any time. Here's how to do it:

List FIVE things you can see. This might be something outside the window, your feet on the carpet, a picture on the wall or a small detail like a shadow on the ceiling.

List FOUR things you can feel. What is the sensation of your clothes against your skin, or a gentle draught in the room? Do any of your muscles feel tight? Or perhaps soft? How does it feel to be sitting, or standing, on the surface beneath you?

List THREE things you can hear. Quiet your thoughts for a moment and notice any sounds that are close (a ticking clock) or perhaps in the far distance (the traffic outside the window; the neighbour's television). Let those sounds be there.

List TWO things you can smell. Is the air fresh, stuffy, sweet? Is something cooking nearby? Can you pick up the fragrance of a perfume or hair product? You could also find something near to hand such as a bottle of essential oil or packet of ground coffee and focus on that scent.

List ONE thing you can taste. Is there a trace flavour lingering from a recent drink or meal? Could you eat something like a mint, sweet or piece of fruit and focus on that flavour?

The Emotions List

We like to list a lot of things: from our goals to our groceries, basic tasks to other people's birthdays. What we don't tend to list, and yet might benefit from most of all, is the changing weather of our emotions. That said, mapping one's moods *digitally* has become an increasingly popular activity and a number of apps are available to help you do just that, such as Daylio or Reflectly. For the digitally detoxing, why not begin instead with a pen and paper list?

This sounds simple but is really rather profound. While we tend to notice big emotional experiences like anger, grief or glee, our smaller emotional experiences can often pass by unnoticed. This is particularly true of our positive emotions. While acknowledging all of our emotions as valid is vital, it can be especially helpful to take note of our positive emotions, because these are the feelings that can be the most fleeting of all. What is more is that research shows how noticing and savouring positive emotions can have a number of 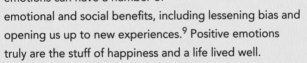 emotional and social benefits, including lessening bias and opening us up to new experiences.[9] Positive emotions truly are the stuff of happiness and a life lived well.

Use the following list as a starting point to identify all of the positive emotions you think you have experienced in the past 48 hours. You are free to add any of your own not listed here.

Alert	Fanciful	Peaceful
Amazed	Fun-loving	Proud
Amused	Glad	Self-assured
Appreciative	Grateful	Serene
Awestruck/ in awe	Harmonious	Trusting/ trusted
	Hopeful	
Close	Inspired	Uplifted
Confident	Interested	Spirited
Content	Joyful	Surprised
Curious	Loving/loved	Valued
Ecstatic	Open	
Elated	Optimistic	
Encouraged		

When individuals try this exercise it is not uncommon to find that they have experienced upwards of 20 positive emotional experiences just in recent days – something that can be both surprising and deeply reassuring. Try it yourself and see. Noticing even five positive experiences is a wonderful insight into where the joys of your life currently lie.

The Strengths List

One list that might serve to motivate us more than any other is a list of our individual character strengths, also known by psychologists as our 'values in action'.[10] These strengths are reflected in our behaviours, relationships, careers, feelings and thoughts.

Researchers in the USA have found that acknowledging and applying our individual strengths in our lives serves to support us both in overcoming times of adversity as well as thriving in times of opportunity.[11] They have identified 24 character strengths that appear to broadly apply across cultures, social groups and generations.

While each of us will possess all of the strengths listed to some degree, we can all probably recognize a number of signature strengths – often regarded as our 'top five' (but you might choose a top six, or ten, or more). You could either choose these from the list below, or take the free survey available at viacharacter.org to identify your top strengths.

Once you have identified your strengths, you might simply write this list out and place it somewhere you will see it often, such as above your work desk or on your fridge. You might take this further by listing some of the ways in which you are already applying this strength in your life, or perhaps ways you would like to apply it.

Appreciating beauty

Bravery

Creativity

Curiosity

Fairness

Forgiveness

Gratitude

Honesty

Hope

Humility

Humour

Judgement

Kindness

Leadership

Love of learning

Loving/Being loved

Perseverance

Perspective

Prudence

Self-Regulation

Social intelligence

Spirituality

Teamwork

Zest & Vitality

The Ta-Da List and the To-Not-Do List

At times, you might have found the to-do list to be a bit of a tyrannical practice. We can become so preoccupied with tasks we *need to do* that we might forget to celebrate what we've *done*, or indeed, what we've (consciously) *not done*. Two uplifting antidotes to the to-do list as we know it, then, are the ta-da list (writing down things we've achieved in a given day, however small and whether or not they ever made it onto the to-do list) and the to-not-do list (things we have successfully shelved for later or struck off our agendas altogether, which is a skill in itself).

While this seems straightforward enough, like with any ritual, we can underpin this habit with a lesser or greater degree of significance. These are lists you may choose to dash off quickly as a way to motivate yourself with past achievements and remind yourself to quell bad habits. Or, you could use these two habits to reflect upon what is truly meaningful to you. Hidden in each of these humble practices is a bigger question: *what is truly important to you?*

The standard to-do list can become clogged with the necessary administrative detritus of daily life (things we might put off for days, weeks or even months if they do not align with our deeper values). Meanwhile, the things we actually spend a lot of our time doing without ever having to put them on any to-do list (e.g. spending time with friends, resting, enjoying a particular hobby) and the things we actively avoid for whatever reason despite numerous outside pressures that we 'should' do them (advance along our chosen career ladder, have children of our own) might tell us a good deal about what really matters to us. Our actual actions, rather than our ambitions, often provide the most robust evidence of our true values. Understanding this can help us make what psychologists call 'self-concordant' choices, where we become increasingly aware of our implicit motivations.[12]

Try the ta-da list and the to-not-do list out for yourself and see if you can distil a sense of what makes your life meaningful and where your real interests lie.

The Life List (or 'Life Calendar')

We might often imagine big life goals, but how often do we *review* the big (and small) achievements and experiences that have brought us to where we are today? The humble list can offer a profound way of, not only plotting what we *would like* to do, but of closely and compassionately reflecting on what we have *already* done.

Researcher and Emeritus Reader at the University of Sussex, England, Celia Hunt, has spent her career researching the complex interrelations between writing, the self and wellbeing. She has proposed a version of the following exercise, calling it the 'life calendar'.[13] She first offered it as a way of facilitating creative life writing, such as writing a memoir. Yet, while few of us will ever formally pen our memoirs, we can nevertheless benefit from an inquisitive journey inward to review the significant moments of our lives – with the help of the humble list.

Here, Hunt's original exercise is reimagined as a life list: a gentle way of gathering together the most significant things we have been through in order to reflect upon, appreciate and, hopefully, understand them a little better (think of this as a bit like a bucket list in reverse). Depending upon what you've been through, this list will likely be therapeutic, motivating, challenging, reassuring, energizing or all of the above. You might complete this in one sitting, come back to it over a few days or week, or even draft out several versions. Feel your own way into this exercise.

Begin by drawing a vertical line in the centre of an A4 piece of paper (portrait orientation) that is lined or unlined depending upon your preference.

ON THE RIGHT-HAND SIDE OF THE LINE

1. Divide the line up into segments that reflect moments of significant change in your life, such as starting school, moving out, travelling, going to university, starting work, an important relationship, etc.

OR 'LIFE CALENDAR'
THE LIFE LIST

THEMES

- Being creative
- Curiosity

- Not trusting myself?

- Making 'sensible' choices to avoid criticism?
- Inside chrysalis

- Butterfly emerges!
- Bravery
- Returning to creative self
- Confidence

── 1988

CHILDHOOD/SCHOOL

- Got into art
- Tough art teacher – (failed A-level)

EXPERIMENTING

── 2007

GAP YEAR

- New Zealand
- Met Jo / first love
- Got into photography

DISCOVERY

── 2008 – 2011

UNI

- Chose business degree
- Long distance with Jo
- Stopped photography

FEELING UNSURE

── 2012...

STARTED MARKETING CAREER

- Moved to London
- Jo break-up
- Joined photography club
- New friends

TAKING RISKS

2. For each segment, identify and list:
- Significant places
- Significant events
- Significant people

3. Next, try to characterize each segment in a single word or phrase such as 'learning', 'voyaging' or 'taking risks'.

ON THE LEFT-HAND SIDE OF THE LINE

4. Now, take an imaginary step back from this personal material, and identify some themes or topics you can see of a more general nature. Hunt suggests things like 'taking on other people's identities' or 'on the road', but other ideas might be things like 'growing up', 'not fitting in' or 'transformation'. You may want to think in terms of a helpful metaphor that ties many experiences together, such as a caterpillar forming a chrysalis and becoming a butterfly.

This list helps to get both a micro and macro sense of the most significant moments of our lives. In completing your life list, be sure to include experiences that you would like more of – those where you felt purposeful and fulfilled for whatever reason, e.g. 'excelled in studies/work' or 'enjoyed big social group' or 'finally travelled to Asia'. Also give yourself space to consider challenges, big shifts or transitions – observing how one event may have led to another.

Once complete, take a moment to sit quietly with your list. What themes or patterns did you notice? Do they thrill you, or perhaps feel difficult? You may wish to take a new blank page (loose or in your journal) to reflect, in a more freeform way, upon the life list you have just created. Write about a specific theme you noticed, or perhaps just your general feelings about the activity until you come to a natural close.

After taking the time to complete some reflective writing in a journal about what these new metaphors might mean for you going forward, you might also like to chat through your list further with a close friend, loved one or counsellor. You may even like to select one or more of the themes that arise as a prompt for a short memoir, or other piece of creative life writing...but it all begins with a simple list.

Correspondence

In the modern world we are more in touch than ever. Unfortunately, this sometimes means we fall out of touch with ourselves. How many mindless messages or emails do you dash off on a daily basis? Probably quite a few. Added to this is the fact that, as much as we now *correspond* with one another, we often fail to truly *connect*. Bringing a little more awareness to your communication habits is a way to change all that, engaging with others in a whole new way.

Humans love to be 'in touch'. We love to be linked, networked – we love, in other words, *relating* to one another. Conversely, we also love our space; we yearn to venture away from the crowd and forge our own path. Thus we live in a perpetual dance between closeness and distance – between trying to be held and trying to be free. Across this gap passes our correspondence.

Writing to others is perhaps our predominant reason for putting words on paper, or piping them out into the digital ether. It is likely that, as you begin to look at your own everyday writing rituals, you will notice correspondence is high on the list in terms of both frequency and volume. It seems, in a way, to matter less *how* we correspond but *that* we do it.

In the deepest sense, this is why words and language exist: to connect us. We share ourselves in spoken and written ways to form a bridge between the world and us. Indeed,

humanity has a long history of innovation with this essential craving to commune. One ancient Roman emperor sent important messages by using metal mirrors reflecting the sun. Our technology may have come a little way since then, but our basic need to communicate remains the same.

Psychologists have a theory explaining our yearning to commune: the *need to belong*. Our desire for belonging is so potent that we spend our lives building relationships and social connections to satiate it. When we do feel we belong, research suggests we experience our lives as being more meaningful – we feel that we matter.[1] Yet this is about more than simply having people around us; the feeling of *belongingness* is a secure sense that we fit in and have meaningful bonds with others.

The way we build these kinds of meaningful relationships is, usually, through *revealing* aspects of ourselves.

Correspondence, then – while it might seem a rote daily habit on the surface – is important. It is how we stoke this spirit of belongingness. We write to one another to be seen and known, and to see and know others; writing is, in a sense, a kind of intimacy.

We tend to think of intimacy mainly in the physical sense. Yet, we might become emotionally intimate with others perhaps never having met them (through emails or social media). This is because intimacy is principally about *sharing* oneself, and through writing things down we can share our inner feelings, thoughts and spirit in the form of sincere words.

Looked at this way, the common phrase that we stay 'in touch' with one another takes on a new cadence, as does the phrase to be 'touched' in the wake of a kind gesture. We experience intimacy that is *emotional*, *intellectual* and *spiritual*, as well as physical.[2] Thinking of our correspondence as a way to practise intimacy with others, then, can help us reimagine how and why we write emails, texts, letters and all forms of written communication.

The exercises in this book will guide you in mindfully writing to others as a way to strengthen feelings of belongingness and thus boost your wellbeing.

Correspondence You're Already Writing

For most of us, our habits of correspondence fall under two main umbrellas: professional and personal. Broadly, there are the work emails on one hand and the social messages or greetings on the other. It is likely that you are in routines with each of these; the exercises in this section will help you explore these in more depth to discover where your habits of correspondence reside, ways in which they are (or are not) helpful for you, and how you might reimagine these habits to reflect your broader values and hopes for your life.

Are your work emails causing you more stress and sleeplessness than they are yielding professional success? Is your instant messaging becoming a chore rather than a pleasurable way to catch up with friends? When we start to look closer, we can see that these routines have the potential to be either deeply nourishing or, actually, pretty draining.

In this chapter we will take the broad view that all of our correspondence – personal and professional – is, at its heart, a space where we *practise relating*. There is that maxim that the way we do one thing is the way we do everything; you might find this holds true of your correspondence. Impatient and terse emails with frustrating colleagues can begin to mean impatient and terse interactions with friends, family and loved ones (or vice versa). Similarly, the best parts of our individual communication style, such as our sense of humour, will tend to apply across everything from our social media posts to our travel postcards to our professional presentations.

The trick to capitalizing on this idea is to think about which of our *virtues* we want to bring to – and strengthen – in our correspondence. Perhaps you would like to become more patient and less irritable. Indeed, all the spiritual practices in the world are of little use if the moment you receive an email from an unaccommodating customer service representative you erupt into a rage. Perhaps you aspire to inner peace but cannot help exchanging reams of strained messages with your spouse or a friend, leaving you perpetually tense and feeling misunderstood. The suggestions in the chapter are designed to help you bring greater awareness to, and develop your highest values through, your correspondence.

By looking at writing you already do to communicate, you are invited here to reimagine your daily habits of correspondence as a space where you can practise awareness, cultivate wholehearted self-expression and experience more joy in your exchanges with others.

The Email

We tend to have a love-hate relationship with email. On the one hand, it has helped us in immeasurable ways. Friends and family who are far away are easier to reach. We can work more easily from home. Shopping and banking and all manner of daily chores have become more efficient. And yet...we sometimes feel hounded by this digital tool.

Email means we are constantly contactable by both those known to us and those who are totally anonymous. We are badgered by newsletters we are sure we didn't sign up to, bullied by marketing bots and forever aware that, even if we step away from our computers, the work messages will be piling up in wait. Some researchers call this kind of cognitive overload 'technostress'. Yet there are ways to tackle technostress and make this communication tool friendlier and less invasive. Some simple tweaks in how we write and receive our digital mail may make all the difference.

TURN OFF NOTIFICATIONS AND 'SELF-INTERRUPT' INSTEAD

One notable study found, perhaps unsurprisingly, that the longer we spend on email the less productive we are and the more stressed out we feel.[3] Interestingly, email-users who choose *when* to access and respond to email, rather than being subject to the bleeps or pings of notifications, are more productive. Keep your email closed and choose a suitable timetable for when you will check and respond, such as once per hour. This may also positively impact your stress level, as it will increase your sense of autonomy about when and how you engage with email.

PRACTISE BOUNDARIES

We often discuss boundaries in terms of our personal relationships, but what of our work boundaries? Because our workplaces often operate in hierarchies, we might feel we don't have the right to state certain boundaries. Yet, even in the workplace, the adage that 'we teach people how to treat us' holds sway. This is a mantra that can be helpfully applied to our emails. Workplace boundaries will always be specific to the individual and the type of work being done, but might broadly look like: not opening or sending emails before nine or after five, adopting a policy of reasonable response times (e.g. two working days), or personalizing your email signature to include your chosen pronouns.

MAKE IT MEANINGFUL

We might feel that email is a place for politeness, productivity and little else. For this reason, work emails are often a mix of small-talk pleasantries and attached documents that need reviewing by the end of the day. Yet one group of researchers found a correlation between life satisfaction and meaningful or 'substantive' conversations (versus 'superficial' interactions).[4] They proposed that, not only does a happy life tend to be a more social life (as many studies have shown), but that we experience even greater wellbeing if those social interactions have *depth*. While this study focused on real-world conversations, we might apply the same logic to our digital interactions. Next time you swap emails with a colleague, take an extra minute to sincerely ask about that book they once mentioned reading or their daughter who has been visiting them, and share something meaningful about yourself in response. Developing this habit of substantive communication may make all the difference to your wellbeing and is a great way to strengthen relationships over time.

The Instant Message

It is easier than ever to get hold of others. That is, at least, in terms of correspondence. We can call, text, use any number of chat apps and be safe in the knowledge that the person we are trying to reach will have their phone close at hand, bleeping at them loudly. Nevertheless, we can feel less like we have a *true* hold of others than ever. When we are with others they are easily reached (and distracted) by the outside world. Our partner checking their phone by our side can make us feel anxious, while they might find our multiple messages to them when apart overly needy. The art of relating via instant message is tricky to get just right.

In psychology, one of the principal theories for understanding how we all relate to one another is the concept of attachment styles – habits of loving and being loved that we learn in childhood and carry into our adult relationships. Broadly speaking, this theory suggests that it is possible to either be *secure* in how we attach to others, or *insecure* in a number of specific ways – with the latter meaning our relationships tend to be much less fulfilling and even leave us feeling stuck in frustrating cycles of misunderstanding. The good news is that we can all learn more secure behaviours.[5]

The theory of attachment styles is useful for understanding *why* we might be messaging, why the habits of another are bothering us and how we can approach this habit more mindfully. Indeed, we can use something as simple as instant messages to observe how we relate to others generally, reverse any unhelpful habits and begin to practise *effective communication* with those we love.

Particularly when tackling a tricky topic or issue via instant message, try out these 'secure' messaging tips:

Be honest. Each message we write is a chance for emotional bravery. Make sure you mean what you say and are not defaulting to game playing. Honesty is the only way to truly get one's needs met in any relationship.

When there is an issue, express your feelings, not their failings (in a way that is specific and avoids blame). For example, 'I need to feel cared for. When you take a day to respond, I feel like you don't care'. Or 'I need to focus during work hours. When you message a lot, I feel stressed'. These are goal-focused and avoid generalizations about our loved ones that may feel, to them, like an attack.

Be confident that your needs are valid. After we click 'send' it is easy to panic and think we have said the wrong thing or asked too much. Know this: you are allowed to ask for your needs to be met in any relationship. If you deny these in the spirit of playing it cool or people pleasing then you are setting yourself up for dissatisfaction in the long run. As long as you have communicated these needs effectively, you can rest assured you have done the right thing.

The Social Media Post

Depending how you look at things, social media falls anywhere on the scale between 'single greatest human invention' and 'the bane of our collective existence'. Such platforms seem to fuel the noblest activism as much as they perpetuate navel-gazing and narcissism, and everything in between.

Social media, if we aren't careful, can be a trap where we find ourselves displaying what Buddhist teachings refer to as three main 'ego strategies'[6] of human beings: our fixation upon

1. Form, or external things
2. Speech
3. Particular states of mind

Buddhists refer to these as the three 'lords of materialism' – called 'lords', perhaps, because we look to them as rulers of our happiness. The problem is that none of these 'strategies' of the ego actually work in the long run, because deeper issues get ignored and fester. Here are some tips for working with these Buddhist principles to help you engage more mindfully in the social sphere.

THREE TIPS TO HELP YOU BALANCE YOUR EGO WHEN USING SOCIAL MEDIA

1. When our egos become too committed to the lord of *form*, we rely on external things as escape routes from uncomfortable feelings, like obsessively swiping

through dating apps to avoid feeling lonely. Meeting new people is a worthy aim, but it's also important to feel comfortable in our own company and not base our self-esteem on how many matches we make.

Try This Instead...Check Your 'Why'

Using dating apps, or writing and sharing via social media platforms like Twitter or Instagram are not bad habits per se, but can become so if practised thoughtlessly. Be attentive to how you feel when you decide to open these apps. Sad? Isolated? Or content? This isn't about judging oneself, but simply about noting what you are feeling *just before* you access social media. This will help you understand why you engage and when, as well as highlighting if social apps are a cover up for difficult feelings, which might be better addressed another way.

2. Overinvestment in the lord of *speech* describes moments when we become righteously indignant about our beliefs, such as in combative Twitter tirades between opposing sides of a debate. The problem here isn't that we *have* convictions, but that our attachment to our own 'correctness' becomes just another way to escape the discomfort of uncertainty. Sometimes it might be best to simply say 'I'll go away and think more about that'.

Try This Instead...Say Less

In the bygone era of snail mail and a telephone box two miles up the road, we all had a lot more time to cool off before speaking our minds. The next time you are tempted to post an emotion-filled or disgruntled message via social media, pause and ask yourself: is it possible to say less? The fact that we *can* be in touch with a running commentary of our inner convictions at all times doesn't mean we *should* – and, sometimes, the less we say the more we can really be heard. Say less on social media, and save the deeper details for your face-to-face interactions.

3. Identifying too closely with the lord of *mind* means we avoid uneasiness or ordinary disappointment by coveting lofty states of awareness (nowadays we might call this 'spiritual bypassing'). In the case of social media, this might mean we retreat entirely from uncomfortable everyday topics around politics or social issues, becoming disengaged in the name of 'love and light'.

Try This Instead...Stay
It might be easy to forget when surfing the waves of the Internet that we are, in fact, engaging with real people and not an obscure assemblage of pixels. Social media can be an important way to bring us together, so make sure that if you digitally detox now and again, or swap your selfies for silent meditation retreats, that this isn't a form of escapism in itself. Remember that it is perhaps the noblest goal of being a human to connect compassionately with others, even when this is challenging. What may be helpful is to approach social media in a balanced and sustainable way, rather than all-in or all-out.

The Greetings Card or Letter

Perhaps the loveliest manifestation of our habit to correspond is the handwritten card or letter. Many of us grew up penning these to our grandparents, perhaps in the form of a thank-you card. You might have carried this habit into adulthood, even if only in a small way – say by sending the occasional birthday card.

We write this way to show we care. This caring form of correspondence may be one of the few times in life when we actually pick up pen and paper as tools to connect with another person. Of course, in the past, this was the main way humans kept their links with one another over great distances. Conversely, today it is easy to know what other souls are up to without having to converse with them at all; their social media profiles provide us with all the selfies and updated statuses we need. Thus there is a soothing quietude to be found in writing by hand, and silently reading a handwritten letter, which is the antithesis to the bold, bright lights of social media.

Cards and letters, because they require us to go a little out of our way, are reserved for those we *really* care about – making them the perfect way to practise what is perhaps one of the most beautiful human virtues: compassion.

One of the key aspects of Buddhism is to practise a compassionate, openhearted sense of connection to all people and beings. This isn't achieved through a unified jolliness. Instead, it is often the result of connecting our own *suffering* with that of others. In this connection-through-suffering, Buddhism teaches, we develop both self-compassion (because we realize our own suffering is commonplace and universal) and broader compassion for humanity at large (because we note that others feel the same pain we do – thus must be quite like us).

An obvious example of this, in the correspondence world, is the get-well-soon or deepest-sympathy card; we send these when someone we know is suffering either physically or emotionally. Yet, *any time* we send a card or letter we have a poignant opportunity to practise compassion.

Unfortunately, we often display a reluctance to relate to the pain of others: we might, for example, actively avoid touchy topics for fear of awkwardness, and stick mainly to superficial niceties. Buddhist teacher, Pema Chödrön, describes true compassion as a willingness to feel the pain of another – in such a way that we are made *equal* in that pain (as opposed to creating a hierarchy of 'wounded' one and 'healer').[7] Sharing our pain is a great equalizer: a way to say 'me too'.

TRY IT

True compassion is what Buddhists call an 'aspiration', i.e. it is not easy to achieve and requires practice, perhaps over a lifetime. Next time you sit to write a card or letter to a relative or friend, practise the aspiration of compassion. When you write 'how are you?' make sure you sincerely mean to discover the answer; ask heartfelt questions, be attentive and recognize the union we all share in suffering (while extending the sincere desire that both you and they be free from whatever particular form of suffering is currently being faced).

The Postcard

The art of the postcard is glorious in its simplicity: a small A5 piece of card adorned with a tantalizing glimpse of our travels. It is scrawled over with a hotlist of things we have been up to, and then hastily left at a hotel reception desk for posting. Whether you travel much or not, this quick way to relate is a treasured habit and one that we can all find time for if we are invested in more mindful correspondence.

What is lovely about the postcard is its spirit of ease and playfulness. You might remember comical seaside gift shop versions from your childhood: a happy reminder that not all corresponding needs to be serious and can actually be a way to wake up our inner child in the spirit of play.

The late psychologist, Donald Winnicott, posited that, even for adults (perhaps especially so), play is a profound way of accessing and exploring our most authentic nature – the unguarded self. Thus playful writing may help us in getting to know ourselves a little better while, hopefully, enjoying ourselves too. Embrace the playful spirit of the postcard with these tips:

Invest in play. Your local stationery shop likely has a rack of brightly coloured postcards with fun patterns, uplifting quotations or bold artwork. As postcards like these are fairly cheap, why not purchase a little stack to send out in place of thank-you notes, or just as a way to send someone a note that you are thinking of them? Think of this as a small investment in a more playful version of yourself.

Get artsy. Much of our correspondence is serious: business projections via email, bills and administrative text messages to our spouse. Light-heartedness, on the contrary, defines postcards. We can embrace this by getting artsy. As a playful child, perhaps you were enamoured of the colourful cosmos of gel pens, bright pencil cases and glitter glue of the stationery shop. Treat that inner child to some special stationery and decorate with doodles, stickers or colourful washi tape – anything your creative younger self would have loved – and for no other reason than to let your guard down and play.

Take five. While sitting to pen a lengthy letter might leave us feeling we have too much else on to even start, popping a few words on a postcard can be completed in as little as five minutes. Yet this has the potential to leave us feeling much more connected than the same five minutes spent on our phones. Keep your supplies close to hand on your coffee table or bookshelf and, next time you catch yourself mindlessly scrolling, dash out a postcard to someone you love instead – a much more creative way to stay connected.

Writing for Confidence

Writing to others can be a pleasure, but it can also be anxiety inducing. Are we saying it just right? Is our grammar as atrocious as we secretly suspect? Will the recipient misinterpret our meaning? If you have ever laboured for an hour on an important work email then you will know that communicating ourselves in the medium of type can be a test of nerve. Yet with a few simple tweaks to this daily activity, we may find ways to drum up confidence in our writing to others.

There is a school of thought in linguistic studies that suggests our struggles to express ourselves in writing of any kind is less about our literacy and style, and more about our identity. 'Who am I?' and 'What do I actually think about this?' are questions we implicitly ask as we translate ourselves onto the page. Writing things down, then, is a chance to get to know *who we are* as much as it is to *make ourselves known* to others; it is about developing authentic confidence in ourselves as much as portraying confidence.

Rosalind Ivanič, Honorary Professor of Linguistics at Lancaster University, UK, has dedicated much of her research career to the relationship between writing and identity. She argues that, when we write, there is a tripartite interplay between our life experience, our sense of self and the reality we are constructing through writing.[1] Between these three elements lies what Ivanič refers to as many *possibilities for selfhood*, i.e. opportunities to grow and develop into who we wish to become.

Becoming increasingly aware of this dynamic between experience, self and world as we write is a helpful way to boost confidence. Try the following exercise and test it out for yourself.

Next time you have a writing task such as an important work email or message to a loved one in which you need to communicate clearly, take a moment to consider the following three questions:

1. *In what ways might my previous experience be impacting this present scenario, or might I be playing out a particular storyline from the past?* This might be as simple as the storyline 'I am not a confident person'. Why is this true? Who told you this, or where did you learn this?

2. *In what ways might my current sense of self be coming into play here?* You might ask: do I feel strong, or am I physically or emotionally drained in some way? Would something help, like a glass of water, a bit of fresh air or ten minutes of stretching?

3. *What is the reality I am constructing/want to construct?* All of our actions, even a simple email, contribute to our reality. If we want to become more confident, we might therefore ask

ourselves what we can *do* to bring this about. 'Become a more confident person' is a huge (and slightly nebulous) aim, but 'write a confident text message in which I set a clear boundary and/or ask for what I need' is easier. Remember that consistent small actions, rather than a single seismic shift, are what bring about big change.

You might use this series of questions to structure the correspondence itself, or jot some personal notes down in answer to each to help you with what you want to say. Writing out your answers to each question in the first instance may help you apply this technique more naturally in future communication.

Correspondence
to Try

Correspondence, as we have already begun to explore in this chapter, gives us the opportunity to either build certain skills or, when undertaken mindlessly, allow them to stagnate (perhaps, even, to erode altogether). Thoughtful, purposeful communication gives us a chance to develop certain virtues – compassion, curiosity, patience, and so on. The exercises in this next section offer new ways of practising corresponding that emphasize building up the best qualities we see in ourselves, or that we hope to find in others. As always, this will likely be highly personal.

Perhaps you are already a very patient person and not much irritates you, but you do tend to have fairly superficial exchanges with others and would like to go deeper. Conversely, perhaps you tend to go very deep in your communication, but you are easily irritated when someone is rigid or disagrees with something you hold to be fundamentally true.

In a typical conversation, we do not always have the ability to step to one side and consider our approach carefully –

maybe we get snappy or are quick to be defensive. Written correspondence, on the other hand, is a slower and more spacious style of staying in touch. When we email, text or write an important letter we have more time to consider our words closely – making it the perfect way to practise interacting in a way that is aligned with our best natures.

Think of any qualities that feel like particular stumbling blocks for you when you try to communicate and begin there, using the following exercises as inspiration.

The *Maitri* Letter

We practise corresponding in all kinds of ways. We rehash old arguments while shampooing our hair and unravel romantic subtexts with friends. One helpful way to practise is to observe our communication with *ourselves*.

Many insights about our relationships with others can be gleaned from the kind of relationship we have with self. In Buddhism, the practice of being with oneself, kindly and directly, is called *maitri*. It is the foundation upon which we relate to others and the wider world: the loving-kindness that starts within.

While a good deal of us will have written, in some form or another, in a diary or journal at some point in our lives, few of us will have written a letter to the self. Yet, in times when our relationship with our self may have become fraught or bumpy (a sure-fire signal that our relationships with others may soon become so) it might be useful to discover novel ways to commune with oneself.

To write a *maitri* letter of loving-kindness to yourself, take your best letter-writing paper and begin a message. You do not necessarily need to have anything in mind to say at first, but address yourself as you would when writing any other kind of correspondence, i.e. 'Dear [Name]'. You may then find one or more of the following prompts useful:

- I have been meaning to tell you that...
- I wanted to remind you...
- I know you have been wondering about...
- I had always meant to say...
- The advice I have for you at this moment is...

This might feel unusual or a bit silly, but it is an important opportunity to model the kind of communication you would like to have with others. This is because, just like we get into bad habits of nagging or griping with others, we can fall into these same bad habits with our own self: not really listening, being short or irritable, cutting ourselves off, limiting our expression to old and unhelpful patterns, etc. Addressing ourselves directly on the page is a way to interrupt these habits, and to develop *maitri*.

When you are done, pop your letter in an envelope, address it and literally post it to yourself. This step is important as it gives you time to forget what was written for a day or two (or longer if you don't post it immediately), offering a helpful distance that allows this contact with yourself to feel like correspondence with another.

EXTRA TIPS

- If you know you are going on a trip, post your letter ahead to the location where you will be so that it can meet you there. This is a good way to 'welcome' your self into that new environment.

- Address the letter to a future self if you know there is something you will be worrying or stressed about in a few weeks or months, and wait until then to open it.

- Describe a current goal and ask your self if they agree that it is a good direction for you. See what feelings arise when you read this goal back later. Excited? Daunted? Use this as a barometer to test if this particular path is something you truly want.

The Mindful Morning Message

Morning practices are powerful. They have the ability to set the entire tone of our day – or, at the very least, allow us to have a small win before breakfast (making us feel better about less productive days). We tend to think of these kinds of wellbeing practices as fairly solitary – perhaps we do some yoga, write in our journal or meditate. Yet, given that social connection is a vital component of our wellness, shouldn't logic dictate that we make this an integral part of our morning practice, too?

If you have friend or relative with whom you keep a regular contact of messaging, ask them if they would like to make this a more focused practice with you, i.e. not in dribs and

drabs as a form of escapism from your work day, but a more intentional way to connect first thing. You could personalize this in whatever way suits you, but here is a basic approach:

Agree a time that suits you both and that is close to waking as possible. Wish the other a good morning and then each share:

Three things that are going really well for you. Have you been eating well? Enjoying a great book? Seeing some success at work? Share these simple joys with your mindful morning companion.

Two things you celebrate in the other person. Stoke the fire of interconnectedness with this person by giving them a pep talk and getting one in return. You might say things like 'I admire your commitment to your job' or 'You always make others laugh'. Anything from the small and specific to broad qualities they possess.

One thing you are committed to getting done that day. Set a doable goal or intention for the day – and then do it first thing. For extra accountability, you might check in with your friend later to let them know how you got on.

The whole process should take no more than around ten minutes. Do not overthink this – just commit to something manageable and enjoyable for you both.

The Tonglen Email

Perhaps one of the most frenzied and frustrating forms of communication is our email – particularly work email. Tense messages from stressed colleagues can, if we are not careful, steer the course of our entire day into our own stress-response that may then rub off onto others (a bad chain reaction in which to get stuck).

In Buddhist teachings, an alternative way to approach such difficult moments is a practice called *tonglen*.[8] This Tibetan word literally translates as 'sending and taking'. It describes an ability to 'take in' the pain, stress or even just disgruntled moments of our selves and others, and 'send out' whatever solace or peace are needed.

The essence of this practice lies in, quite simply, pausing in the moment of meeting stress, staying open to this discomfort and breathing in this unwanted moment into the limitless spaciousness within the self. As we exhale, we visualize sending out relief and happiness, to self or other, in whatever form is needed.

Tonglen may be just the antidote you need if you find your email Inbox to be, on occasion, a stressful space to spend time. Formal *tonglen* practice has four stages. Here is a quick guide to applying these steps in your email habits (or, really, any kind of correspondence you would like):

   1. Next time you open an email that leaves you feeling piqued, take a moment to pause in stillness – just noticing. Stay soft and hold a moment of unconditional openness to your experience.

2. Following this pause, visualize the energy of this stress or discomfort, letting go of any story attached to it: does it feel hot? Spiky? Heavy? Claustrophobic? Simply notice the texture or quality of the feeling.

3. The third step is the main essence of the practice: breathe in what is unwanted in this moment, and breathe out whatever relief is needed. If a tense colleague is aggressive about a task left unfinished, breathe in their stress, as well as your own, and breathe out peace for the both of you.

4. The fourth step (which can be combined with step 3 if you like) is to widen this circle of compassion to include others who might be suffering in the same or similar ways. Breathe in their stress into your limitless interior, and breathe out what is needed – calm, peace or even something specific such as a warm tea, a hand held or restful sleep.

The fundamental power of this practice is that it does not *resist* experience. It is not a meditation to be practised in a quiet corner of our homes, but an 'in the world' tool that helps us face the everyday challenges of life. Instead of tensing against difficult moments, we surrender to them, and we hopefully find, with gradual practice, that our capacity for peace is a lot less limited than we thought.

The Gratitude Letter

A great many of us will be familiar with the practice of the thank-you note. Some kindly soul bestows on us a gift and we return their gesture with a few words of gratitude. This tradition is both well-mannered and a reflection of our appreciation for another keeping us in their thoughts. The issue, as with many mannerly practices, is that this can become rather shallow.

Gratitude is an emotional experience and not one that can be faked. Only *we* know when our gratitude is sincere. Yet, when this is so, the shift in our perspective on things can be quite radical. Several landmark studies in positive psychology have looked at the effects of gratitude on our wellbeing, demonstrating benefits from improved mood to increased resiliency in the face of disaster to better cardiovascular and immune-system health. Of the various gratitude practices scientists have studied, one of the most common interventions is the gratitude letter.[9]

TRY IT

1. Choose a person you care for deeply, but to whom you perhaps do not express your thanks enough.

2. Write this person a letter, by hand, explaining what they mean to you. Include specific things you recognize they have done for you, and why you are thankful. Write around one side of A4.

3. The important third step is to deliver the letter in person and read it aloud. Remain mindful as you read, pausing to observe your own feelings and the reactions of the other person.

4. Stay to discuss any feelings that arise, and remember to leave the person with your letter when you go.

Interestingly, the effects of various gratitude practices have been found to be less strong and even non-existent when sampled by people from collectivist cultures.[10] For these groups, helpful behaviours that support others are more deeply woven into daily life as standard, and thus are less of a pleasant surprise as they tend to be in cultures with more of a self-focus.

If you come from more of a collectivist background, keep this in mind and perhaps adapt the exercise to emphasize a different feeling or emotion, such as compassion or hope – whatever feels 'needed' for you to connect more deeply with a particular loved one.

Whole Person Communication

A lot of our troubles in communication can come from forgetting that we are not just cognitive, rational beings – but feeling beings. Many of our convictions and decisions are emotion-driven rather than logic-driven, though few of us might want to admit to this. Whole-person communication – whether by email, social media, text message or in a letter – is a forgiving form of relating that acknowledges the person in front of you as much in terms of their feelings as their logic.

Here are some tips for trying this yourself:

Be curious about the experience of others. So many of our interactions go wrong because we cease to be curious and instead make defensive assumptions. Miscommunications happen, but unless we *seek clarity* we will repeatedly fall victim to incorrect conclusions.

Ask questions. If there is a secret to good correspondence – and good communication more generally – it is learning the art of asking good questions and truly listening to the answers we receive. It is better to ask *one good question*, and hear the answer, than talk for hours and get nowhere closer to unity on a given subject.

***Reconsider** how you ask.* You may be thinking, 'well, I ask loads of questions' – but what form are these questions taking? (We all suffer from bias, bouts of sarcasm, tetchiness, and misunderstanding the motives of others). Perhaps you ask things like:

- 'You don't really believe X, do you?'
- 'You've done X again, haven't you?'
- 'You aren't really thinking X, are you?'

These are what we might colloquially call 'loaded' questions. In such instances, we are not really asking a question. We are being accusatory. The blame has been laid forth before the other person can even answer, and we may find that they behave defensively in response.

Let others (and yourself) be less logical.
People think, speak and act as a result of their feelings – yet so often we judge others by logic alone. Embracing our *feelings* as well as our bright ideas is at the heart of whole person communication (in contemporary terms this is called 'emotional intelligence'). Ask those with whom you correspond not just 'what do you think?' but 'what do you feel?' and see the difference this makes to your communication. Remember to allow *yourself* to be a feeling being – or whole person – too.

Notes to Self

While the notion of talking to oneself is often disparaged as a bit, well, *odd*, most, if not all, of us practise the inaudible art of the note to self. This curious pastime allows us to commune with ourselves in the briefest of ways: from a scribble on a napkin corner to digital curating of our thoughts via an app on our phone. Seldom cogent to others, our notes can nevertheless harbour deep meaning. Hidden in this habit is a desire to relate to oneself that, with closer exploration, is an important and powerfully reassuring practice.

There is a familiar sense of urgency we get when an idea or insight pops into our mind. We know we will forget if we don't quickly commit it to paper. Annoyingly, this often happens at the most inconvenient times. Just dropping off to sleep? Here – have your best notion yet about how to tackle that tricky project at work. In the shower? Here you have a perfectly phrased sentence to communicate to your partner why you have been acting out of sorts. These kinds of contemplations are rather unwieldy. They arrive, not when we are ready for them, but instead when we relax into thinking about something else altogether. Thankfully the note to self is the perfect way to preserve even the most disorderly of deliberations.

Capturing notes to self – whether in a dedicated journal, on a flock of coloured Post-its or in the Notes app on our phones – is something many of us do. Philosophers and psychologists alike have come up with many theories for why we might put our thoughts into words in this way. Perhaps one of the most interesting theories of these is that words are an organizational tool.[1] The special remit of words is to extend the sphere of our thoughts from beyond the confines of our minds and onto the extra space of the page. We write these notes, in other words, to give our selves *room to think*. It is almost as if we do not have space in our heads for that one important thought; we require the spaciousness of the page.

Spaciousness is a feature of Buddhist teaching – a state of being towards which we might aspire in sitting meditation, and an antidote to the many ways in which we often tense, resist and become rigid in the face of daily ups and downs. The space of the blank page, then, is both a useful practical device and a wonderful metaphor: it offers us the physical space to organize ourselves, as well as the more metaphysical sense of spaciousness that our stressed-out spirits often crave.

What is more is that notes to self allow us, with their features of brevity and ease, an important opportunity to *just be*. In the quickly scribbled note we release expectation on ourselves to perform in any particular way – our penmanship is rarely called into question, nor is our insight or idea judged too harshly. Thus the elegant *transience* of these jotted-down notes helps us bypass the many trappings of our egos.

Indeed, the note to self is compellingly distinct, as writing habits go. We compose these briefest of scribblings without the structure or thought-through-ness of a list, without the intention to share it with another, without the depth of reflection reserved for a journal and, often, without the sense of any further plan having taken shape.

These are tiny snapshots of our inner life which, taken out of context, likely make no sense at all. Notes to self are, perhaps more so than any other writing form, little 'word selves' that we leave in our wake. They are a small bit of us at our most real.

This makes for a wonderfully pure and free sort of writing practice; there are no particular demands we put on a note to self. We don't imagine someone will come along and judge our handwriting, denigrate our transitory musings or rain on this particular parade of ponderings because, simply, these are 'just' notes to self. That 'just' is important. That 'just' sets us free from obligation, and our ego; we are allowed the freedom to *be*, just as we are, on the page (or napkin corner), in a way that few other writing forms offer.

Notes You're Already Writing

Notes to self tend to have little logic, structure or stylistic approach. They are pure bursts of thought that we know will pop like bubbles into the ether if we do not enshrine them in a more concrete form. These notes might eventually lead to longer lists, detailed plans or compelling creative feats of imagination...but, in the first instance, they often lack all sense, elegance or grammatical structure. Thus, we can practise the craft of the note to self in all kinds of ways, several of which we will explore in this section (though this is by no means exhaustive).

This ritual is akin to compiling curatorial notes on the goings on of our lived experience: a guide to the exhibition of *us*. Through our notes, the content of our days and weeks can be pieced together in a hastily captured book of restaurant recommendations, poetic insights or prosaic reminders to take the bins out. What sorts of notes do you currently capture?

Despite a seeming incoherence, notes to self often signify a profound thought, important reminder or sacred bit of information we want to treasure. This way of writing is important to us for all manner of reasons – we just may not have thought much about it until now. In this first section, you are invited to explore and hopefully recognize some habits you had not previously noted, as well as tips and ideas for bringing more meaning to this everyday tool.

The Reminder

Perhaps the most valuable feature of the note to self is its usefulness as a memory device. Where else, when travelling on the bus or between meetings at work, would we capture those important thoughts about what needs doing, but in the form of a hasty note?

In the past, one might have kept a physical notepad and pen on one's person to collect such important warnings. Today, it is typical that we tap these into an app. However you collect up your reminders, it is common for this practice to revolve around day-to-day chores such as prompts to pop to the post office, or cues to pick up the phone and make an important appointment. It is a way of gathering up tasks, in other words, that we often *don't really want to do*. Hence, we avoid them. Hence, we need a reminder as a prod into action.

Yet, instead of allowing the reminder to become a mindless self-shepherding exercise, we can use these kinds of notes to self to become *curious about our laziness*. We can get to know rather than condemn ourselves. Buddhism teaches that we have three principal forms of laziness as human beings:

1. We resist the discomfort of a task
2. We feel hopeless about a task
3. We become resentful of the task[2]

We will likely discover each of these if we scan our eyes across our reminders – but the good news is that Buddhists do not see these traits as bad or shameful. We can simply observe such habits in order to better know ourselves and, perhaps, even increase our productivity. Next time you write a reminder, ensure you stay curious and open to your very human inclination to *avoid the task* by considering the following:

We avoid tasks because we crave comfort. Things that put us out in some way, such as uncomfortable chats on the phone or queuing to send a parcel, are liable to rouse avoidance. They *inconvenience* us – and the more convenient we believe our lives should be, the more irritated we are likely to become at minor hassles. **Get curious about your need for comfort.**
Ask: does this reminder make me uncomfortable in some way? How so? Is this discomfort real, or does it dissolve when I try to capture its specific qualities? How might I

make this task feel more comfortable for me through my own thoughts or actions?

We avoid tasks when we lack heart. This brand of laziness, in Buddhist teaching, is actually a sense of hopelessness. We avoid tasks, or begrudgingly push through them, all the while feeling that things are a bit meaningless. *Put your heart back in it.*
Ask: where might I find meaning in this reminder? What gives me hope that my actions have significance? Rather than force myself to complete this as an 'obligation', how can I kindly reinterpret things and access a sincere willingness, or sense of choice in the matter?

We avoid tasks when we think or say 'I don't care'.
The final type of laziness is a resentful laissez-faire attitude, where we upgrade from lacking heart to active defiance. A good way to think of this is as though we have a slightly spoiled inner child or moody teenager, who is huffing at the very idea of the task. *Make it cool to care.*
Ask: how might I avoid wallowing in this feeling of defiance? What am I resisting – really? If this is my inner child reacting, how does my inner parent want to respond?

When we look closely at any one of these forms of resistance about getting something done, without judgement or self-criticism, we tend to find that there is not much substance to it. With a moment to pause and reflect in our writing, we might find ourselves becoming a lot more productive as a result of our reminders.

The Idea

The feeling of having an idea is wonderful. It can be a kind of transcendence – an illuminating 'a ha' feeling traditionally characterized by the light bulb switching on above our heads. Yet if you have ever been just dropping off to sleep and told yourself you will remember that compelling thought that has popped into your mind, then you will know how nigh on impossible a skill this is: that is without, of course, the help of a note to self.

We often treat our journals, emails or letters as sacred places where we are afraid to make a mess or misrepresent ourselves in some way. In those writing forms, we may wish to project ourselves as a perfectly complete portrait, and not in the more honest sense: a person in process. What is so helpful about the scribbled idea as a note to self is that it is so low stakes – we may even just throw it in the bin tomorrow morning. This freedom helps us break free from self-censorship.

Indeed, our brief idea notes that we jot down may actually be one of the *realest* forms of writing about ourselves that we can do, because we aren't trying to prove anything or fix upon any rigid vision of things. We allow for chaos, contradiction, change and – therefore – we allow for growth. These little notes, or word selves, are 'us' in that they contain our thoughts, but also 'not us' in that we do not attach to them too deeply. They therefore offer us an infinitely more honest way of writing for happiness and wellbeing.

TRY IT

If you have ever found
the concept of a journal
daunting, or tried and
found you were crippled by
self-censorship (a common
reaction to the
'specialness' of a
clothbound journal) try
reframing this practice instead into a
Brief Ideas Notebook. Keep this notebook to hand by
your bed and treat it in the spirit of the humble note to
self. Allow one- or two-word entries, half-finished
sentences, torn-out pages and scribbled-through bits. By
granting yourself the freedom of contradiction and
disorder, you might just find you have your best ideas yet.

The Insight

Arguably qualitatively different to the idea is the insight or
musing. While an idea might have the sparkle of being
entirely unrelated to anything already going on in our lives,
an insight is the kind of note that adds a fresh perspective
to something already unfolding. Indeed, one of the most
common ways that insights arrive is when we are reading a
jolly good book.

Where, when deep in the pages of a compelling non-
fiction title or enjoying a beautiful novel, does one capture
one's insights? Why, in the margins, of course. This form of
note taking has been so widely practised over the years

that there is even a term for it: marginalia. Famous writers known for their marginalia include Oscar Wilde, Isaac Newton and Sylvia Plath – so you are among eminent company if you, too, scribble a note to self in the margin.

THE ART OF MARGINALIA

In his famed poem on this topic titled, simply, 'Marginalia', Billy Collins calls these missives 'footprints along the shore of the page' – and few other descriptions so precisely capture the mindful quality of this simple art form.

If you have tended to balk at the idea of imprinting your insights on a book in this way, here are some tips:

Pencil, pen or even a highlighter? For some, using a pen will feel far too permanent – and brandishing a highlighter a true scandal. For others, pencil might just be too feeble a footprint. You might find a highlighter helpful for textbooks, but not novels. Find your own unique way to make a mark with your marginalia – just not in library books!

Review now and again. What is lovely about this practice is that we begin to build a much more personal library. Were anyone to one day inherit our book collection, a piece of us would go with it. Return to your old books now and again to reflect on your own marginalia and what it means for you – perhaps adding new notes to old – and gradually granting yourself an overview on your own individual archive.

And, of course, read the marginalia of others.
It is always tempting to purchase a pristine new copy of
any book, but, when we do, we deny ourselves the
privilege of peeping into a past owner's pointers on the
title. There is a lovely sense of connection to a wider
reading community when we glimpse marginalia of old
– so don't deny yourself this pleasure by only buying
brand new.

The Observation

Observations arise most often when we are on the move
– when the setting of our lives is in transit. We spot a new
restaurant that has opened nearby, or see someone with a
hairstyle we like and may wish to emulate. These sorts of
thoughts also get captured in our notes. They tend not to
have the intelligence of an insight, or the forward
momentum of an idea. Rather, observations are those

'huh' moments of spotting something that we have an opinion on, but may not ever do much about.

The problem with observations is that they can, if we are not careful, cause us to get *too* caught up in the external world – we might follow trends obsessively, check the local or national headlines constantly, and find we are forever fretting over things far out of our control. This excessive stimulus can, over time, make us feel rather anxious and burnt out. What might help, if this sounds like you, is to practise the Buddhist art of groundlessness.

In Buddhist teachings, groundlessness means setting ourselves free from grasping or clinging to any external thing too tightly. It is letting things be, just as they are, without letting our ego get too mixed up with it. We watch the world passing by (and we equally *relate* to people and things as compassionately as we can – this isn't a form of escapism), but we do not *invest our identity* in anything, like the news or a passing trend. An analogy for this is that our experiences are like dust settling on the mirror of the self; we might continually wipe away the dust, or we might acknowledge that perhaps there is, in truth, *no mirror there* upon which the dust can settle.

Every time we make an observation we have the chance to notice our groundlessness, practise just letting things be as they are and avoid potential burnout. One way we might do this is through a mantra. Next time you make an observation you are compelled to write down, take an extra moment to follow with a written mantra on groundlessness. A typical Buddhist version might go as follows, but you can make up your own using words or a particular metaphor that feels resonant for you.

Mantra for Groundlessness: Groundlessness, greater groundlessness, complete groundlessness, awaken, so be it.[3]

The Quotation

The words of others can be supremely motivating, and we love to capture them in our notes. While our own reminders, ideas, insights and observations all have compelling weight in our lives, there is nothing quite like the motivating phrases said by others much wiser than we are.

More than being just motivating, however, the quotations of famed minds and inspiring folk do something altogether different, but equally helpful: they humble us. Humility is not one of the sexiest virtues, and as a result we often find it is in short supply in the world. Everyone we know – and we can probably include ourselves here – seems about to launch their own business endeavour, 'rebrand' their identity on social media, or is poised to produce something big and important that they want to tell us all about. When we read the pithy quotations of others from the past, we are invited to stop awhile and, perhaps, wonder where little old us fits into a wider, wiser, collective.

Humility should not be confused with self-deprecation. In reality, we are not that great, but we are not that awful either. We are loveable, if sometimes misguided, human beings. Collecting up the quotations of others teaches us that we still have things to learn; that we will, in fact, always have things to learn.

The Greek philosopher Socrates knew all about this. He is oft quoted as having mused 'I know that I know nothing'. While there is no evidence that Socrates ever uttered this exact phrase, it does highlight the spirit of much of his philosophy: the idea that we should seek those wiser than us, and engage in dialogue with them, so that we might learn more about the world and about ourselves.

TRY IT

Next time you capture a quotation you love, consider entering into a dialogue with it on the page. Ask, simply, 'Is this true?' to begin, and record a brief answer. Next, you might ponder 'In what ways is this potentially untrue?' Continue on in conversation with the pithy quotation and you will be conducting your own version of Socratic dialogue: a method of getting just that little bit wiser by staying humble about things we might not actually know all that much about.

Writing for Calm

When a child is upset or concerned we tend to console them, not only with a hand held tightly or a hug, but also with our words. We say gentle things like 'there now' and 'it's alright', or 'you're okay' and 'I'm here for you'. As adults, we sometimes need similar reassurance – and writing can provide just that. A few gentle words on paper can provide a remarkable amount of calm in some of our most stressful times. Notes offer, in a sense, a quick way to talk with ourselves about what is going on – and to check we are okay.

Another feature of notes in particular is that we can employ them instantaneously, like a plaster on a cut, for our most urgent thoughts or unsettling realizations. In this sense, notes can be a useful calming technique for our inner first-aid kit, because they are quick at hand when we need them.

Tap into Trust

Many emotions and feelings come into play when we write. Yet perhaps one of the most calming of these that we can choose to tap into is *trust*. Life is not always easy. It would be nice if it were, but there are times when we simply cannot feel joy, or levity, or gratitude. At these times, what we can do is trust. Trust is a deeply positive, yet gentle, emotion. It asks only that we surrender to the current of things.

Most of us can relate to the feeling of life being a bit like an uncertain, sometimes perilous, path we must follow. There are always peaks and troughs; there are always monsters and magic helpers. Looking at life as a journey in this way is perhaps one of our greatest

shared metaphors. It crosses cultures and provides a helpfully unifying narrative for the human experience (which is, of course, also wonderfully diverse). Note-taking, when looked at within this metaphor, is a kind of 'captain's log' – a way of both charting a course and understanding what that course might mean for us up ahead. It acts as a reminder that the journey we are on is not an easy one, nor was it ever meant to be, but it is one on which we can *trust* ourselves to learn and grow.

Tapping into trust in our writing is useful because it can widen our view of a situation, helping us surrender to a bigger picture of things, rather than tense against the moment. In instances of great anxiety, what tends to happen is we act in 'fight or flight' mode. Rather than considering the situation with cool rationale, we go into alert mode, zoning in on the perceived threat, our body pulsing with the adrenalin it thinks it needs to fight off a predator.

It would be unrealistic to think we can avoid this state altogether. So much of contemporary life seems almost *designed* to arouse this response in us (work, commuting, vast superstores, car parks...). The world is a stressful place. What we can choose to do, however, is respond with trust.

Write Yourself a Trusting Note

Next time you find yourself in a frazzled moment, pause to write down what you trust. Use the following prompt to guide you, and then just write a sentence or two in response. Over time, you might collect up these notes to form a 'log' that reminds you of how many unnerving situations you have overcome. Equally, you could discard these notes, *trusting* in yourself that whatever wisdom you drew upon in that moment is carried within you.

This is what I trust...
Example responses:

'I trust that I am loved and supported'

'I trust myself to make the best decisions for me'

'I trust that I can overcome this'

'I trust that this will pass'

Notes
to
Try

Notes to self are so distinctively sporadic that it feels odd to require any particular shape or sense from them. We should, rather, enjoy them for the way they wriggle free of the constraints of order and reasoning. Nonetheless, it never hurts to be inspired by new ways to approach old habits – even those outside of discipline and design.

Notes offer a way of writing for wellbeing, better organization and a boost to our personal resources – yet in a way that allows for freedom, spontaneity and delight. We can grow bored with prescriptive dictates about our wellbeing. Perhaps we feel we have heard it all before, or we are just tired of the rules and regimes of 'adulting'. The note is the antithesis of that – notes offer a way to explore our most authentic inner musings, savour the best bits of our lives, affirm who we are, find deeper meaning and cope with uncertainty – all by, perhaps counter-intuitively, embracing the ephemerality and fleetingness of our experience.

Use this section to look at your note-taking in a fresh light, turning to these new habits and rituals (or getting inspired to create your own) as a way to feel better. These notes take little time or planning, but can nevertheless have a big impact.

The Meditation

Nowadays, the word 'meditation' evokes a quiet, sitting pose, while we contemplate the present moment. However, another definition is our *written (or spoken) thoughts on a subject*. Perhaps the most famous example of this can be found in the writings of the Roman emperor and Stoic Marcus Aurelius – his *Meditations* are often referred to as one of the earliest-known examples of a personal self-development 'journal'.

Reimagining your notes to self as meditations on life and experience gives these writings a particular significance. These brief notes act as a gathering of our thoughts into a greater story – one that helps us make sense of things. Creating a meaningful narrative for our lives is a core human need. If we lack a 'story' that makes sense, this isn't just unpleasant but can lead to burnout and even depression.

For many, religious practices offer a comforting 'story' about what happens (we understand things as 'God's will'). Yet in increasingly secular environments it can be tricky to find this sense of purpose in our day-to-day life. Writing down our meditations can therefore offer a way to develop our own philosophy for living, within a relatively simple practice.

While a long-form journal-writing practice might offer something similar, the note form makes this practice quick and simple and low investment – avoiding us feeling overwhelmed by the task.

TRY IT

What follows are some tips for writing your own meditations. You might begin a dedicated journal for these, or establish a section in an existing journal or daily diary that you are writing. You could also set this up in the Notes app of your phone – whatever feels like a convenient way for you to organize your reflections.

To begin, you might capture daily or weekly meditations under a few themes such as 'Work', 'Relationships', 'Health', etc. Over time, sub-themes might emerge. Remember: this is *your* developing philosophy for living, your gathered wisdom and your advice to self, so tailor the practice to suit you.

Meditations are personal writings to promote clarity. These types of notes are not designed to be read by others (Marcus Aurelius seemed not to intend his to be read – sorry, Marcus), so make sure you can compile them somewhere private.

Meditations are short (we might call them the original 'note to self'). A meditation of between a sentence and a short paragraph is ample. Keep things succinct and each entry focused on a specific point.

Meditations have a self-development focus. Use yours to reframe any particular challenges as opportunities to develop strengths and values, e.g. 'Although my relationship right now is particularly challenging, this is giving me the opportunity to hone my integrity and self-care practices'.

Meditations are actionable. While a journal might act as a space to philosophize, lament and ponder at length about life's lessons, a meditation should ideally be a short call to action, e.g. 'Next time my work colleague is rude or short with me, it is my choice to not react and preserve my own peace'.

The Savouring Note

The practice of gratitude is a cornerstone of wellbeing practices as wide-ranging as ancient religions and the most contemporary self-help. Less familiar, perhaps, is gratitude's close cousin – savouring.

When faced with life's most difficult experiences, each of us will have a list of our own coping habits and ways to reassure ourselves. A practice like savouring turns this idea on its head: it exists in the spirit of strengthening our sails *before* our ships hit stormy waters. Savouring is a practice of more mindfully experiencing life's most wonderful moments. Writing can help.

Savouring is well suited to note form rather than, say, a list or journal, precisely because these moments are often very brief. What is more is that the benefits of savouring are many. Researchers have identified that savouring can positively impact our relationships with others, foster creative problem-solving and even improve physical health.[4]

TRY IT

If you want to give this practice of mindful note-taking a try, the following tips may spark ideas on how to begin.

The simpler, the better. This practice is not about celebrating only exotic trips or birthday parties, but of observing the more quotidian joys of an ordinary day: fresh coffee, sunshine and a kind word from a friend. Make sure these things get written down.

Sharpen your senses. Savouring is all about awakening our senses to everyday joys: cool morning mists, crisp leaves under foot, dappled light through a tree, the scent of baked things and the taste of sweet tea...Make sure you use all five senses when writing to savour.

Be ready. Think of your pen and paper as a kind of butterfly net – poised to capture fleeting moments of joy and contentment. The closer to hand your pen and paper, the easier it will be to preserve these moments. Notebook and pen in the car glove box, anyone?

Notice what is brief. The butterfly analogy is also useful for thinking about the transient nature of these moments, because a butterfly is often gone before we have even noticed it. This is why writing down what we savour is so useful. Look for the things that pass by quickly and savour those (a child growing up, a seasonal change, etc.).

Share what you savour. While there is no need to share your writing itself, research indicates that telling others about how we have experienced positive moments makes us happier.

The Affirmation

Writing a note to self can offer a powerful form of what psychologists call *self-affirmation*. As much as notes offer a method for organizing and recording our thoughts, this is also a way of us saying 'I am here! I matter!' Researchers have suggested that self-affirmation is a process of boosting our self-resources to cope with challenges, because affirmations help uncouple the self and the threat.[5] Self-affirmations can therefore function as part of what we can call our 'psychological immune system'.[6]

From time to time, most of us will sense certain threats to the self, whether real or imagined, which an affirmation of our values in writing may counter. Indeed, writing down our values in this way has been shown by researchers to boost what psychologists call *self-efficacy* – or the feeling of 'I can' – because this way of writing can focus us in on the resources we have at our disposal to meet life's challenges.[7]

TRY IT

Suggestions for this type of writing from researchers are very specific, with guided writing prompts such as:

What gave you strength today? How did this become apparent to you? Describe your thoughts and feelings.

You could try this as a long-form exercise in its own right, or adapt this self-affirming way of writing to your daily note-taking habits. For the latter, next time you scribble a friendly reminder to your future self, experiment by adding an affirming sentence to the note that focuses on your strengths.

For example, you may be taking down a private memo that you would like to bring up in an important work meeting. To this you might add the sentence:

My opinion is important and my creativity will give me strength today.

You may find that even a simple affirmation like this can bolster your resolve in demanding scenarios.

The Aphorism

While an affirmation centres on our own experience, the aphorism does something a little different: it widens our lens to include the experience of others. Simply, an aphorism is a fancy word for a general observation. More complexly, aphorisms capture broad truths about being human. This can help us feel connected to one another rather than isolated.

> 'When the heart weeps for what it has lost, the soul laughs for what it has found.' – Sufi aphorism

> 'You have come here to find what you already have.' – Buddhist aphorism[8]

Few of us may capture quite such profound jottings in our day-to-day notes. Yet a helpful way to understand the aphorism is as a practice predicated on our search for *meaning* in life. This is because aphorisms help us zoom out from the quotidian and consider a larger perspective.

What makes your life meaningful? It is a big question – and one we might forget to ask, or even actively avoid, because the sheer scale of it scares us. Yet meaning is fundamental to our wellbeing. This idea is explored in the book *Man's Search for Meaning* by Viktor Frankl, a psychotherapist imprisoned at Auschwitz and other concentration camps during the Holocaust. Throughout this harrowing experience, and that of those around him,

Frankl became impassioned about what it is that powers humans towards survival. He concluded that it was meaning: a why, or reason, to carry on.

Of course, there is no quick fix for finding meaning. It is a subject that spans the width and breadth of any life. Meaning exists in many guises, from what psychologists sometimes call 'ultimate meaning' to 'meaning of the moment'. We cannot snap our fingers and expect meaning to materialize in our lives. What we can do, however, is adopt a *meaning mindset* – and we might well be helped in this endeavour by the practice of the aphorism.

DEVELOPING A MEANING MINDSET

The meaning mindset is an idea posed by researcher Paul Wong. It is an alternative to the success-orientated mindset adopted by many of us (think of the 'American Dream'). A meaning mindset encourages us to seek experiences and situations that are significant, and not to be principally driven by material desires. A meaning mindset describes how far meaning motivates us – but this may come naturally to us or be a conscious choice.

Wherever you find meaning – in friends, family, creativity, a 'calling', learning, nature, in big or small doses – keep this in the forefront of your mind by penning a daily or weekly aphorism.

TRY IT

The idea of writing aphorisms of this kind is to allow what is meaningful to you to motivate you, not only the material. To really capture the spirit of the aphorism, it may also be helpful to phrase these as general truths (rather than using the first person 'I') – giving you that sense of connection to others who may be feeling the same way.

Researchers have found that writing in the second person (i.e. to 'you') or third person (i.e. 'she/he') can avoid us becoming entrapped in our individual emotional experiences – particularly if we are anxious. One study found that, while first-person reflective writing promotes a valuable release of emotions, the second person can offer a greater sense of self-supportive dialogue, and the third person may foster a more objective view of things.[9]

Try these prompts for penning your very own aphorisms, and see if they work for you (or adapt and design your own):

What matters most to your spirit is...
You find meaning in...
She resolved to...so that she could...
He felt unsure about...but remembered that...
When a person feels challenged, they can...

Use these ideas to carefully widen your focus and draw your attention to the deeper significance of your daily experience, rather than getting too caught up in the material things.

The In-between Note

Humans perpetually seek resolution, conclusions, firm answers and fundamental truths. This is an admirable trait in many ways; we are endlessly curious and have an insatiable appetite for knowledge. Yet, in our personal lived experience, this yearning for fixed or definitive answers can often do more harm than good. This is because we are chasing something that is, frankly, impossible; life is too full of uncertainties. Thus, it is usually much more helpful, and healthy, to see oneself and one's experience as in process, or *in between*.

Buddhists similarly advocate for embracing the uncertainty and transience of life. They train in avoiding becoming too attached to anything – physical, mental or spiritual. Buddhists practise acknowledging this groundlessness or 'in-between-ness' as fundamental to life; any time we 'fix' on something, an idea, person or situation, we are hiding from a deeper truth (and setting ourselves up for a fall).

You do not, however, need to have months of psychotherapy or convert to Buddhism to benefit from exploring your experience in this way. Enter the in-between note. This practice relies on one simple concept: throwing your note away. Our lists, correspondence, diaries, etc. are so often enshrined, saved and revisited. This might leave us feeling, at times, trapped in a web of words we have inadvertently weaved in the aim to define and communicate aspects of ourselves.

The power of the note is to free us from this web, because, simply, *we can discard it when we are done.* If you find personal writing a challenge because of its candid nature, then this practice is perfect for you.

TRY IT
The in-between note values the idea of in-between-ness. It is all about practising seeing the self as a process, not a finished masterpiece, and in a way that is liberating. For that reason, there are only two simple steps:

1. *Write down what is on your mind.* This might be something that is bothering you or feels challenging. Pen just a sentence or two about how this feels and what you think it means. Alternatively, it might be something about which you feel excited or desirous.

2. *Throw the note away.*
Whether the thing you have written about is ostensibly 'good' or 'bad', the act of discarding it is a ritual in not attaching ourselves too tightly to the 'situations' of our lives. This is a reminder that we are always in between, and to exist *in process*, rather than cling to any particular circumstance.

To make this ritual more eco-friendly you might want to cut up some old envelopes or other waste paper and keep a stash of these recycled pieces to hand for your new practice.

Journals and Diaries

Whether or not you are in the habit of keeping a regular diary or journal it is likely that at some point – maybe as a child or teen – you have had a go at recording the goings on of your life. At particular periods, perhaps in hardship or times of angst, personal writing of this kind can feel very important – yet its time-consuming nature means it can fall by the wayside when life gets busy. This chapter looks at ways of making this a soothing ritual and daily joy, rather than an extra chore or purely emergency measure.

Many forms of writing challenge us to wrangle into words specific details about ourselves and our experience – but perhaps none more so than the journal or diary. In these long-form, private ways of writing we can confront inner conflicts, process what has happened to us and come up with new ways to be ourselves. Indeed, although we tend to talk about the 'self' as one thing – a single soliloquy that runs the show from within – diary and journal writing show us that things are often rather more complex than this. The experience of being, or having, a 'self' is closer to what some psychologists call having a *society* of selves, incorporating all the voices we have picked up from our relatives, peers and other influences.

The Dutch psychologist, Hubert Hermans, believes that the self is more accurately described as 'many "I" positions that can be occupied by the same person'[1]. In other words – the self is a lively *conversation*. We are in discussion with ourselves all the time – and, as Hermans describes, this dialogical aspect of our nature 'can be felt when writing a diary'.[2]

In a diary or journal, we can view our many internal 'I' positions as they play out; they become a part of the external world (the page in front of us) and thus we can get a clearer, more objective handle on them. Put another way, in writing we become *readers of ourselves*.

Thus, diaries and journals are powerful practices. They scaffold our very relationship with who we are. So much of our success and survival in life depend on the ability to hear our own needs and trust in ourselves enough to set about getting these needs met. Indeed, the main principle of a journal practice is to become adept at exactly this. You might have long had the impulse to engage in personal writing for this very reason: to get to know who you really are. Or, perhaps you did something like this in childhood but left the habit behind. Maybe you have dabbled in keeping a diary but have always given up and never quite known why this habit would not stick. This chapter is an invitation to explore some common ways to journal, as well as to try out some new ways.

It might be that the task of a journal or diary feels rather onerous. This way of writing takes a degree of dedication and commitment. Some may find this begins to feel more like a chore than a delight. If so, it can be useful to reflect on the self-soothing quality of writing – to frame this personal writing as offering a space, not to tell yourself what to do or how to be, but simply to listen: to gently 'hold' how you feel.

From the daily diary, to the liberating practice of freewriting, to integrative ways of writing about our experiences, to creative ways of writing in a journal – this chapter offers twists on these established writing habits. Each suggestion aims to be flexible and positive rather than burdensome. Try out a few to find what works for you – and reconnect, or connect perhaps for the first time, with the practice of personal writing.

Journal and Diary Writing You're Already Doing

It is easy to see why we are driven to write in diaries and journals: life is confusing and, at times, full of such varied stimuli that it can feel as though our heads are spinning. We juggle family commitments, social pressures, tough work projects, keeping healthy and all the while try our best to get some downtime to simply relax. Many of the roles we play in life require us to be not-quite-ourselves. We are professional and ambitious at work, self-sacrificing with loved ones, tummy sucked-in and determined at the gym...it is no wonder that many of us are drawn to that space where we are required to be nothing more than our plain old unremarkable selves: the pages of a journal.

Whether or not you have ever formalized the process of personal writing, we have all at times been tasked with writing about ourselves. As school children we learn to write about what we did at the weekend. At college or university we might pen critical commentaries about a project. In our professional lives we may have been asked to keep a reflective account of our work. This is a unique feature of human beings: we are preoccupied not just with the business of existing, but also with the *story-ing* of our existence.

The first exercises in this chapter ask you to look a little more closely at the most common forms of personal writing, as well as suggesting some helpful ways to engage a little more mindfully in these habits. There are practical tips as well as some research insights to help you understand why you write the way you do about your day, your travels or your professional and personal goals. Explore them and see if anything surprises you, or makes you look at this ritual differently – hopefully with renewed awareness of what these ways of writing offer.

The Daily Diary

Perhaps what springs to mind for most of us when we think of a diary is what we might call a daily diary – the kind of volume in which we detail, in linear order, the quotidian goings on of our lives. Many people begin these types of diaries as children. There are tiny hardback journals one can purchase from stationery shops in bold colours, perhaps adorned with animal characters and complete with tiny lock and key.

To record our lives in this way is a form of self-investigation – and thus a way of developing self-knowledge. In a daily diary, we write a story of ourselves to ourselves. Indeed, we might begin to regard this 'story of self' in overly simplistic terms (i.e. as a logical, linear experience with a 'beginning', 'middle' and 'end'). This simplistic view does not capture the many complex levels of human experience. Indeed, as the literary scholar Paul John Eakin once wrote, what we call self is 'a mysterious reality'[3] – it does not necessarily match up with the 'stories' we tell about it in a diary. To make this practice more helpful, then, we can consider the more diverse kinds of self-knowledge available to us.

Late psychologist Ulric Neisser described five principle ways that we know ourselves – all of which provide useful points of perspective for daily diary writing. Try writing a whole entry for one of these on a given day, or check in with each daily:

WHAT IS IT LIKE TO BE IN YOUR PHYSICAL BODY? (the Ecological Self)

You can think of this perspective, in the poet Mary Oliver's terms, as the 'soft animal' of the body. Animals have an ecological self in that they are sentient: they feel sensation including pain. They cry, mourn, play – all without telling any kind of 'story' to themselves about any of this. We are animals too, not just 'thinkers'.

Write a diary entry from the wonderfully mindful perspective of your physical body: what has it felt today? What experiences were important to your body? Just describe the sensations without applying any meaning or 'story' to the experience.

WHAT IS IT LIKE TO BE YOU IN RELATION TO OTHERS? (the Interpersonal Self)

You might think of this as your 'social self' – the outside version or 'front door' of you. We have interpersonal selves from the time we are babies, so this is not about complex conversation with others – anything from a hug to a handshake are ways that we exist in relation to other people.

Write a diary entry from the perspective of your self in relation to others: how have you been relating with others lately? How do others relate to you? What does it feel like to be a self in your family, romantic relationship, work team or society?

WHAT IS THE BROADER NARRATIVE OF YOU? (the Extended Self)

This is the past-present-future self. The narrated or 'storied' self. Psychologists say we develop this at around seven years old, when we begin to get a sense of who we have been and where we are going, as well as who we are in the immediate moment.

Write a diary entry from the perspective of your extended self: what past experiences are affecting you?

What are you excited or worrying about for the future? What *part* of your 'story' are you living right now and how might this fit into your wider story?

WHO IS THE YOU THAT NOBODY ELSE KNOWS? (the Private Self)

Others can intimately know us, but there is always an interior realm that will never be fully grasped by another person – no one can hop inside our head, after all.

Write a diary entry from the perspective of your private self: what is deeply true about you that others do not see, and that is perhaps even quite hard to put into words? Is there a helpful metaphor for that part of you? What does this private self feel?

WHAT ROLES DO YOU PLAY AND WHAT DO YOU BELIEVE ABOUT YOURSELF? (the Conceptual Self)

This is the self that exists in abstractions and outwardly determined ways. Concepts of ourselves might include being 'mother' or 'executive'; or, we might consider ourselves 'spiritual' or 'atheist', 'artist' or 'homemaker'. It might be that we are 'intelligent' or 'good looking'.

Write a diary entry that examines your differing self-concepts, or choose just one: who is the you that's a 'good employee' or 'disorganized' or 'sporty'? Remember that not all our self-concepts are true – and that you can examine and interrogate which are helpful or less helpful for you.

Are there some concepts you might retire, or reimagine? Could you put two or more self-concepts in dialogue on the page, for example your 'reliable' self in conversation with your 'impulsive' self? What would they have to say to one another? What might they each want you to know? You might set this out with speech marks, just like dialogue in a novel, or perhaps use two colours of pen to differentiate.

Freewriting

While you may not know it as freewriting, many of us practise scribbling down our thoughts in a free-form burst on the page, whether occasionally or regularly. The practice of freewriting involves a kind of letting go to see what's there when we put pen to paper. Formal freewriting is usually done in a timed surge or by using a set number of pages. It might start from a gentle exercise, but often from no prompt at all. The only rules are that you keep writing and do not concern yourself with grammar, spelling or punctuation. You must simply keep your hand moving.[4]

When trying freewriting, you might experience a very meditative release in which you write something deeply felt that you didn't realize was there. Alternatively, you might find yourself writing, 'I don't know what to write' over and over again, or several pages of complete gobbledygook. Both are valid. Freewriting involves no attachment whatsoever to outcome. It is a warm-up – like a freeform shaking of the limbs before a structured physical exercise regime. The only endeavour is to let go, see what is there and let it be there.

GENERAL TIPS

Find the time that works best for you. In her book *The Artist's Way*, Julia Cameron prescribes a particular version of freewriting: three full pages every morning as a way to clear the path for creativity.[5] You might find it more helpful to write in the afternoon or evening. Try out different times over several days and see what works best for you.

Freewriting is typically done by hand rather than digitally to aid its meditative quality (i.e. less chance of distraction from incoming messages, temptation to surf the web etc.), but you might experiment with writing electronically if that works best for you.

Freewrite on loose sheets of paper or a cheap A4 pad. The less 'special' these pages are the freer this practice will feel.

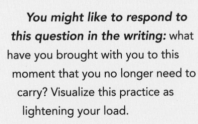

Set a timer for five, ten or twenty minutes. Timing ourselves helps offer focus and sets a safe boundary.

You might like to respond to this question in the writing: what have you brought with you to this moment that you no longer need to carry? Visualize this practice as lightening your load.

As a technique, freewriting is not only useful as a form of personal writing – next time you are stuck on any writing project, even a professional one, set a timer and do a freewritten version. You can edit later, but switching out of our more critical, self-censoring or high-achieving mode gives us helpful space to actually hear what we think.[6]

The Reflective Journal

Far from being solipsistic navel-gazing, reflective ways of writing encourage us to relate in more helpful ways with others, because they allow us to understand our own preconceptions, defences and anxieties. Writing researcher Dr Gillie Bolton notes that reflective practice 'challenges assumptions, ideological illusions, damaging social and cultural biases, inequalities, and questions personal behaviours'.[7] In other words, this way of writing helps us *respond ethically* to what happens (i.e. in line with our highest values) rather than *react obliviously* (i.e. out of habit or conditioning). To 'react' is often knee-jerk, whereas to 'respond' involves considered choice. This is what reflective writing offers: the chance to adjust our autopilot settings and stay firmly in the driver's seat of our lives.

You may be familiar with reflective writing in professional situations such as annual performance reviews in which you are invited to critically assess your work process and outputs. In daily life reflective writing can offer a space to acknowledge how our subjective experience impacts our way of being in the world. We can learn to acknowledge our privilege and take responsibility for our shortcomings, because this practice encourages a critical perspective on our own actions across time. It is often tempting to be clipped or brief in a diary, and it is equally as easy to ruminate or over-indulge our woe. Reflective journal writing helps us strike this balance between skirting around our flaws or drowning in self-pity, guided by introspective-yet-kindly questions such as 'What went well?' and 'What needs work?'

TRY IT: RESPOND RATHER THAN REACT

The following reflective questions are adapted from Bolton's advice in her book, *Reflective Practice*, and offer a way to get started with this type of writing for either personal or professional development. You might begin a dedicated reflective journal to explore these types of questions, or incorporate them into an existing writing practice.

- How do you tend to behave when faced with a challenge? What about when things go well?

- How might you value the perspective of others on a situation you currently face, however different these others are to you?

- How might these others perceive you? What might be their feelings and thoughts about things?

- What can you change about how things are? Is it possible for you to counteract seemingly given social, cultural or political structures? How might you adapt to what you cannot change?

THERAPEUTIC WRITING The backbone of emotional wellbeing is *healthy emotional expression*. For many of us there has probably been a time (or two!) when our emotions have felt overwhelming. Therapeutic writing is a freer form of reflective writing that assists us in processing this. It involves thoughtful, cathartic introspection, often in relation to specific incidents from our personal lives.

You might write this way in bouts and bursts when needed, or as a more formalized regular practice. Importantly, this way of writing is not necessarily about 'feeling better' but about 'better feeling' – the aim is not to rid yourself of these emotions, but rather to experience them healthfully. Next time grief or shame or disappointment strike, in your writing you might ask yourself, simply: 'How can I better feel this emotion?'

The Travel Journal

One particular occasion when many of us are prompted to write is when travelling. New places and environments inspire us because they offer a fresh perspective on things. We step away from the humdrum activities of the everyday and, suddenly, our senses come alive with novel sights, sounds, smells and sensations that we want to capture. To do so, we turn to words. We might use a travel journal to capture the view from a train window, to note vivid details that will help us to remember a beautiful hiking location or to chart the route we take through a country.

Travel journals are useful because we often over-estimate what we are going to remember about a particular experience. Anyone who has ever found an old journal and had the experience that they were reading the words of another person will know this. This revisiting is good for us. Studies show that experiences tend to make us much happier than material things. Having a record of these may help us get more for our money, because we can savour the experience again and again. More recent research has hinted that, even more specifically, it is having experiences *with others* that offer the biggest wellbeing boost.[8]

If you keep a travel journal, make sure you aren't just capturing details about the sunrise over the Taj Mahal, the fresh scent of the Alps or the creak of the boats as you punt down Venetian canals. Record the people you meet in these places, as well as details about those with whom you visit. Write about the eccentric hotel manager, the young man you get chatting to in a café or the companion you have taken with you...what about those others makes the trip special and memorable? In-jokes? Local knowledge? Philosophical conversations? Romance? Let your travel journal hold all the best parts of the trip by making sure that it includes how you shared the experience with other people.

The Bullet Journal

If long-form personal writing has not always been your thing, perhaps you have tried your hand at bullet journalling instead. Ryder Caroll, pioneer of the bullet-journal process, developed this system to radically focus his attention after a diagnosis of attention deficit disorder. In his own words it was a way to 'concentrate on the right thing at the right time' – and he developed this 'cross between a planner, diary, notebook, to-do list, and sketchbook' to be 'a practical yet forgiving tool' for getting things done.[9]

The bullet-journal method works by *rapid logging* of the future, the current month and the present day with a series of elegant, bulleted lists of things we want to accomplish. Tasks, events and notes are indicated by a dot, circle or dash respectively. Important tasks are marked with a star.

Yet the flexible, forgiving and mindful nature with which this process was created seems at times rather lost in translation in the ways this tool is used in the mainstream. Its focus has, in places, become rampant self-discipline rather than self-forgiveness. Thus it might be useful if you already use this practice to balance the regimented energy of the bullet journal in the following ways:

Don't go to war with yourself. Any productivity journal can be at risk of becoming just another way to get in a fight with yourself. Unfortunately, self-improvement can sometimes be synonymous with self-rejection and it is important that we protect ourselves from this. Make sure to check in with yourself and ask: am I working with, or against myself in my bullet journal? Celebrate the ways in which your bullet journal is helpfully motivating to you, but remain attentive to the ways it might be telling you that on your less motivated or productive days you are less than worthy.

Give yourself a 'messy page' now and again. As soon as any practice becomes too rigid and we begin to see ourselves striving for perfection, it may be helpful to temper this urge with the opposite energy: mess! If your bullet-journal practice has become a hive of efficient yet somewhat draconian order, try tempering this by including, with equal excitement, some messy pages. Use these for doodles, daydreaming and making mistakes without repercussion, outside of the official bullet 'system'.

Acknowledge your life – and yourself – as a work in progress. The spirit of allowing messy pages is an invitation to gift your self *the right to be a work in progress* – not figured out, but figuring it out. Not having sussed things, but sussing things. This will avoid you falling into the trap of self-rejecting. Remember that it is possible to be both ordered and messy, both logical and passionate. Living well is not about perfect consistency, but about holding juxtapositions intelligently.

Journal
and Diary
Writing
to Try

It is easy for any wellbeing ritual to go stale after a while – and journal writing is no different. Even a seasoned diarist can become bored by repetition of a task, even those that feel deeply fulfilling to start with. Therefore, this second half of the chapter encourages you to move a little way out of your comfort zone with this writing habit.

Perhaps you are somebody who writes religiously at the end of the day about every meal you ate, every person with whom you spoke or every thing that happened – and you have slowly begun to find this task lacks the pizzazz it once had. Maybe you have kept a therapeutic journal for a while but find you tend to rehash the same old stories and that this has begun to feel more like rumination than any kind of consolation.

Here you will find tips and tricks for writing in ways that outwit self-censorship and integrate different shades of yourself. You are invited to weave your most positive and life-affirming emotions into a journal practice. Finally, you are encouraged to flex your creative muscles and dance between the practical and more poetic realms of fact and fiction. All these ways of writing have one thing in common: they shine a fresh light on an age-old practice.

The Internal Censor Audit

When we are small children we are very honest. We lack inhibition and are able to be purely ourselves for a short while before the world begins sculpting us with its judgements. Too soon, our parents begin to tell us 'no'. Our teachers tell us 'that's wrong'. Bullies tell us 'that's stupid' or laugh at us. As we mature into adulthood, lovers and employers alike reject us, we fail at certain dreams and we make embarrassing mistakes. All this to say that, by the time we reach the page of a diary or journal, we can be rather timid about expressing who we are. We arrive laden with shame and doubt that can be tricky to shake.

A way around this conundrum is to get to know our internal censor, because a journal is not likely to be very helpful for us while we are hiding or ignoring our true natures. With a close examination of exactly who this censor is, what they are saying to us, as well as how they might be hindering us, we can begin to leave them behind and – perhaps for the first time – truly be ourselves on the page.

WRITE TO YOUR INTERNAL CENSOR

1. Begin by asking, simply, 'Who are you?' and allow this critic to answer.

2. Based on the response, write a portrait of this person – as if they truly were a living, breathing being. You might even sketch them out. What would they wear? How would they move around?

3. Next, write a list of typical things they say to you, e.g. 'You are too self-indulgent' or 'You will just make a fool of yourself here' or 'You can't possibly write *that!*'

4. Spend some time in conversation with these statements on the page. Write down what you want to say in response to your inner critic.

5. Tristine Rainer writes in her book, *The New Diary*, that we can sometimes 'make a deal' with our internal censor by promising to throw the writing away if they will let us express what we truly feel.[10] See if this works for you by writing on loose sheets of paper rather than in a bound journal.

6. Return to these exercises whenever you feel you are struggling to be honest in your journal practice. Hopefully, with time, you will need them less and less.

Integrative Writing

We sometimes feel scattered. The many demands on our time and distractions of the day-to-day can leave us exhausted and stressed out. We might feel anxious, spread too thin and worn out by trying to be all things to all people. Sensible self-development is about *integrating* these varying shades of self – not rejecting them. Sure, some parts we like more than others, but all are valid and worth recognizing because, if we don't acknowledge them, they are liable to rear up in all kinds of unconscious ways. Much psychotherapy operates on this principle, but we can begin to integrate in a personal journal too. Integrative writing is a conscious practice of bringing together diverse parts of self and experience on the page.

TRY IT: 'YES, AND...' INSTEAD OF 'NO, BUT...'

As we endeavour to draw the various threads of ourselves into helpful cohesion with integrative writing, perhaps the simplest way to start is with what's known as the 'Yes, and...'

technique. Let's say you write a problem you are having in your journal, or an aspect of yourself that you don't like all that much. Instead of trying to 'get rid' of or resist this issue (i.e. by writing 'No, not this, but this...'), reflect instead upon what might also be *simultaneously* true by writing 'Yes, and...'

Some examples might be:

- I hate this project at work. *Yes, and...*I am also learning a lot.
- I am always so late and unorganized. *Yes, and...*I also try hard to show up for what I care most about.
- I can be difficult to love. *Yes, and...*I am also extremely lovable.
- I am uncertain about the future. *Yes, and...*I also feel excited.

This is a helpful way to keep a journal entry going in a productive direction, rather than getting stuck on a problem – safely holding our experience rather than rejecting parts of self. You can do as many 'Yes, and...' sentences as you like.

This capacity to hold competing truths within our selves leaves space for what, beyond the obvious and immediate, is also true. It is a simple but very important skill: preventing us from rejecting or going into battle with any part of our experience. We simply acknowledge what's there *and* recognize the growth that is happening too.

Writing for Self-compassion

Compassion for ourselves does not always come naturally. Many of us demonstrate great care and concern for others, but can be remarkably cruel in the words we use with ourselves. Internally, we might say things like 'You always screw up like this' – words we would not dream of saying to anyone else.

If you keep a journal of any kind, or write regular notes to yourself in your phone, think about how kind the words you say to yourself have sounded lately. Might you be a little nicer? A little less abrupt? A little gentler? One of the leading researchers in self-compassion, Kristen Neff, has developed a body of research around this gentler way of being with our selves. Mounting evidence shows how self-compassion supports both our emotional and physical wellbeing – and so is a habit worth getting into.

Neff suggests several ways in which we can foster this more loving relationship with who we are – including supportive touch, such as placing our hands on our heart, or monitoring our critical self-talk. A foundational pillar of this practice, for Neff, is writing things down. She suggests a daily self-compassion journal, in which we can practise three things: mindfulness of our emotions, understanding of our common humanity and self-kindness.[1] You might begin a journal specifically for this purpose, or explore these things in your regular writing practice. Here are three tips to get you started:

1. *Mindfully affirm the tough stuff.* A commitment to self-compassion will not make your difficult feelings disappear. When you judge yourself, feel shame or experience guilt it is important not to further berate yourself for having these feelings! Instead, begin mindfully holding space for those thoughts by writing about them without judgement. You might write: 'I was so embarrassed by that mistake I made at work – it made me feel foolish and as though my colleagues might think I'm bad at my job'.

   Simply state what you feel as closely as possible, without minimizing or dramatizing what happened.

2. *Reflect on your shared humanity with others.* All people have experienced failures much like

yours. Everyone faces difficulty. Congratulations – struggle makes you human, not a robot. Write about the ways in which your difficult experience connects with the experience of others. You might write: 'It is okay that this happened, because I don't have to be perfect. Everybody makes mistakes sometimes. Life can be difficult for us all'.

Allow yourself to be reminded that everyone experiences shame, turmoil and regret at one time or another. No human being is immune.

3. *Practise self-kindness.* Once you have acknowledged what is difficult and observed how difficult feelings make you an ordinary human being, you can then express some kind words. Imagine writing a supportive message to someone you love very much – how would you comfort that person? You might write: 'I understand this feels tough, but go gently with yourself. These feelings will pass. You are still worthy, even when you mess up. Maybe you can ask for help next time. Expecting to achieve everything on your own without error is pretty unreasonable'.

Adopt a warm, reassuring voice – but, importantly, in as authentic and heartfelt a way as possible (if this feels too forced, perhaps leave the writing and return later when it can be truly genuine).

The Dream Diary

Dreams offer an interesting window into our inner worlds
– and are therefore worth exploring closely in a diary.
Where some exercises and writing prompts may leave
us uninspired, our dreams are our in-built inspiration
catalogue for our writing practice: a way of recognizing
what might be affecting us without our logical awareness.

In *The New Diary*, Tristine Rainer writes that diaries offer 'a
bridge between dreams and the waking life'; they provide
'a space of your own creation where the subconscious and
the conscious mind meet'.[11] Rainer sets out many ways
that we can begin to diarize our dreams, but three of these
are perhaps most helpful for the beginner just getting
started: description, reflection and maps of consciousness.

Describe the dream. What was happening? Who was
there and were they simply themselves, or merged with
someone else in some way? What were the main images or
sensations you remember? (If these have no logical order,
you might simply list them.) At this stage, do not attempt
to analyse what happened; just record it.

Reflect. Once you have captured the detail of the dream, begin to look at it closely and unravel its insights with some interpretation. Allow yourself many possible interpretations by writing: 'It is almost as if...although, it might be that...or, this could even suggest...' You will likely soon settle on an interpretation that feels most true for you, but the point of this reflection is not to *correctly* analyse your dream. There is, of course, no *one* correct analysis of any dream. Whatever interpretation feels most helpful for you in this moment is the right one.

Maps of consciousness. Dreams are so distinctly visual that, sometimes, reflecting in words will not be enough. If that feels like the case for you, use your journal to sketch images from the dream (rough approximations and stick-people are fine – you do not need to be an artist). You might use cartoon-style dialogue bubbles to capture words or meanings. If your map draws out any additional significance, you might then do some further reflective writing about this. What do these sketches show you?

The Positive Journal

Our negative emotions can get rather a lot of airtime. A lot of our self-talk can be critical. Many of our professional interactions can feel like complain-a-thons or gossip-based bonding and a good deal of our personal social interaction can revolve around venting about our frustrations and many obstacles. We derive a real sense of solidarity in shared suffering, because it validates our own. Positive moments can, conversely, feel difficult to share; celebrating our own successes and wins can feel self-indulgently boastful or unfeeling in the face of others' less-than-happy experiences.

Sadly, this can result in shame and cynicism building up around our positive self. We might have hidden a joyous moment when a friend was suffering because we didn't want to 'show off'. We might have covered up an

achievement in the presence of a colleague because they were experiencing a setback. There is a lovely empathy inherent to these moments, but there is also a good deal of self-betrayal.

This is where a positive journal practice comes in – it is a way to be with your positive self on the page, without shame or cynicism. It is a method of working intelligently and sensitively with the most life-affirming aspects of being you: your hopes, your awe, your interests, your gratitude, and so much more. It is an exploration of positivity, not a prescription of it. The practice is not about seeking outside for shiny accolades. It involves, instead, recognizing ourselves as having a great well of resources within us: our positive emotions.

TRY IT: GET TO KNOW YOUR POSITIVE SELF

Finish the following sentence starters with a fresh page or two in your existing journal – or begin a brand-new dedicated positive journal. Keep in mind that there is no 'rule' that you must be perpetually jolly in this writing; it might be tricky to access certain aspects of who you are. This is an exploration that can take time and gentle patience, not an exercise in faking it until you make it. The idea is to begin by drawing on any experiences you might have had where you felt the following emotions (e.g. perhaps you felt a lot of joy at a particular time in childhood), then consider how you have been experiencing the emotions lately (e.g. perhaps you feel a lot of interest in your work) and finally think about ways to get to know these positive parts of yourself better going forward (e.g. experience more awe by getting out in the natural world).

- I once met my [joyful/hopeful/proud/grateful/loving/interested/awe-struck/serene] self when I...
- I meet them now when I...
- I could get to know them better by...

Note that you might use any number of positive emotions and feelings beyond those suggested (e.g. your contented self, your peaceful self). Work with those that most resonate with you.

Having written a journal entry for each of these 'selves', you can now revisit them whenever needed. You can also invite them to your regular journalling any time you are facing a particular challenge, or want to record something that is going well in your life. Things you might write in your daily journal are:

- The message my [joyful/hopeful etc.] self has for me right now is...
- If I welcome them into this situation they will offer me...
- If they were to take action here they would...

The Creative Journal

The personal journal can tend to bring out our more playful sides, because its private nature means that we (hopefully) avoid fear of judgement from others. We can capitalize on this by bringing *creativity* to our journal practice. Creative journals can take many forms; they might act as a kind of vision board, a scrapbook, a sketchbook or even a place for poems and short stories as well as life goals. Most importantly, however, they should be a place to *revel in inefficiency*. Many journalling methods revolve around productivity and efficiency, but creativity is inefficient by design. As soon as we are too prescriptive or regimented, we can stunt any real imagination and shut out possibility. Invite imagination – and therefore greater possibility – into your journal writing with the following idea:

TRY IT: WRITING AUTOFICTION

Autofiction is the term for what, on the surface, is a contradictory way of writing: autobiographical fiction. It involves writing that is not quite true and yet not quite made up. Crossing the boundaries of fact and fiction in a journal may seem worryingly unhinged – until you think about how much of our experience is, essentially, 'made up': our anxiety will have us worry about umpteen possible future disasters that have not actually happened – and may never happen; similarly our version of events of things that do happen will always be fallible (i.e. we forget details, misunderstand, fill in the blanks...). Autofiction is a way of capitalizing on this 'made up' quality of experience by both daydreaming possibilities and reimagining the past.

Add a character to a real situation who might have helped, or might help now. Set things in a different location. Add dialogue you wish was said. See if these experiments help you understand things in a new way (e.g. opening your eyes to something you needed in the past, that you might gift to yourself now).

Extra tips for your creative journal
Get some distance with the third person. You might write about yourself as 'the parent' or 'the employee'. Switching to this detached style invites creative thinking in a situation we might be finding tough – it becomes less about 'What should I do?' and more about what should that person do (and we are often so much wiser and more forgiving towards others than to ourselves).

Create a 'cut-up' or 'blackout' poem. Snip out individual words or phrases from a newspaper or magazine and rearrange into a piece of poetry to stick inside your journal. Or, use a marker to black out all but a few poetic words in a column and paste that into your journal.

Write in a genre or hybrid genre. What if life were an action thriller or a romance? How would things be different in a tragi-comedy? Experiment with creating stories from your experience, e.g. turn an incident at work into a scene from a mockumentary. Might this help you see the funny side of something that otherwise feels overwhelming?

Goals
and Plans

Humans are goal-orientated. We love to *strive*. Strive for the better job, the next relationship, the new house (or car or outfit or other material object we desire). This can become rather wearisome. Yet, more conscious goals that prioritize our wellbeing just as much as our productivity can be helpful. These kinds of goals and plans ensure that we are navigating our ship in the right direction, but with joyful determination rather than interminable struggling.

The desire to set goals and make plans is one that is deeply bound up in the human experience. Our ancient myths and stories all contain tales of individuals who set off on enchanted journeys – sometimes chosen, sometimes forced by circumstance, but always with a goal. Yet if we have learned anything from these narratives it is that things do not tend to come off exactly as planned. So why do we set our hearts on certain chains of events if we know we are not guaranteed to succeed? Perhaps this is because part of the joy is in the planning itself.

As researchers in the psychology of goals argue, goals are at the very heart and essence of 'what it means to be human'; behind our penchant for planning is a 'desired end state' towards which we strive, but goals also offer purpose *in the moment*, i.e. they are our 'reason for doing and thinking';.[1] Goals and plans sustain us in the now, because they give our efforts – our thoughts, feelings and actions – meaning and direction. They provide a sense of predictability where things might otherwise feel quite chaotic – and this can be especially true when we write them down.

There are many established goal-setting hacks and techniques, however it is important to note that what fits for one person will not necessarily fit the next. We might set goals related to anything from our health to our career, from family, hobbies and books we want to read, to countries to which we would like to travel. We might also record our goals in many ways – they may pop up quite naturally in our day-to-day forms of writing: in our lists, our correspondence, our notes or our journals. Alternatively we might hold a handful of sacred, overarching life goals that we keep tacked to the notice board. Maybe you set flexible yearly and monthly goals (which leave room for manoeuvre). Perhaps you use a different word altogether – such as intention – to capture a more mindful process-oriented kind of goal.

Any philosophy of goal-setting needs to be a personalized one – just as any writing practice is personal – and it can take time and honing to get it just right. Regimented and systematized goals might feel comforting to you, or they might feel like a scratchy sweater you are keen to take off. Take a moment now to see if your goals *feel good*. Is goal-setting enjoyable, or does it make you tense? Is the process exciting, or daunting? You might close your eyes and observe any physical responses you feel to the idea of goals (tight shoulders, butterflies, clenched jaw). Our bodies carry a good deal of wisdom if we take the time to listen.

Remember that your goals and plans, like your life, are your own. If, as psychologists say, goals are our reason for doing and thinking – then it is certainly worth our serious focus and attention to check we have got them right. Use this chapter to further explore some of the ways in which you might have already tried to direct your behaviour into certain goals and plans, while also hopefully picking up some new tips to try.

Do remember, though, that it is important to approach any goal with humour and light-heartedness – after all, there is that adage that life is what happens while we are busy making other plans. Settle in and take some time to explore, joyfully and mindfully, your own plans and goals, becoming excited about possibility rather than wedded to certainty.

Goals
and Plans
You're Already
Writing

In the modern day, it is perhaps fair to say that we have become rather obsessed with goal-setting. Social media is awash with proud announcements of #goals that set us up to want everything from idealized bodies, to idealized boyfriends, to idealized be-your-own-boss careers, to idealized boating holidays. We demand that our jobs, relationships and even daily coffee be utterly joyous, passion-driven and delightful. This can all begin to feel rather relentless.

Perhaps you have set new year's resolutions to have perfectly toned abs, or maybe you regularly set SMART goals for your professional life. Maybe you prefer the pictorial motivation of a vision board awash with yachts and power suits, or the regimented structure of timetabled chores and meals to make every moment of your family life Instagram-worthy.

While it is a wonderful and deeply satisfying part of human life to have big dreams and ambitions, we can sometimes get rather caught up in getting what we want and forget about the joy that is hidden within the day-to-day striving itself. Use the exercises and ideas in this section to reframe some of the goals you have already been writing down and see if you might make them a little more mindful and a dash more joyous.

The Resolution

At the beginning of a new year, many of us write down eager promises to ourselves that we call resolutions. Despite our ardent commitment to these goals, we can be unruly when it comes to following them through. The reason for this unruliness is not always clear. They are our goals, after all – against whom are we rebelling but ourselves? Perhaps, simply, we make them the wrong way. We miss out the important step of analysing the very thing that will make these goals doable: our level of motivation to achieve them. Goals or resolutions are just words on paper if we do not have sufficient drive to go after them.

Researchers often distinguish between what's called intrinsic motivation (coming from an internal source) and extrinsic motivation (coming from an external source)[2]. To illustrate, you might be intrinsically motivated to partake in your favourite hobby – you do it for the joy of it and need zero encouragement. Conversely, you might be extrinsically motivated by a deadline at work – you do it because you have to and need encouragement.

It's important to note that neither intrinsic nor extrinsic motivation is 'good' or 'bad'. Both have their uses. What is important is awareness of the specific type of motivation we experience around any particular goal, if we hope to succeed.

TRY IT: WRITE DOWN YOUR MOTIVATION, NOT JUST YOUR RESOLUTION

When you next decide to set a resolution, ask: what's motivating you? If your goal is to get fitter (a common resolution!) consider how motivated you feel. Are you doing it because a friend recently got fit and you want to show you can do it too, or to attract a new partner (both extrinsic)? Are you doing it to feel better and lighter in your own body, or to equip you to do more of the fun and physical activities that you love like running or skiing (both intrinsic)?

If you only have intrinsic motivation, you may lack the get-up-and-go of real accountability, whereas if you only have extrinsic motivation it's unlikely that you will feel any true joy in actually achieving that goal. For any future resolutions you make, first write a few points on what's motivating you. Try to integrate both intrinsic and extrinsic motivation, and you will be much more likely to see yourself succeed, and much less likely to be unruly.

The SMART Goal

One of the most widely used goal-setting techniques is the SMART system. It dictates that we set ourselves goals that are: **S**pecific, **M**easurable, **A**chievable, **R**elevant and **T**ime-based. You may well have written some of these as part of professional development reviews with your manager, or on your own in pursuit of a particular ambition. SMART goals are very useful but can, at times, feel rather dry. What is worse is that they might not always get us what we want.

As Daniel Gilbert sets out in his book *Stumbling On Happiness*[3], we humans are notoriously terrible at actually knowing what will make us happy in the long term. Gilbert cites research suggesting that we commit fanatically to things in young life (from favourite music to favourite foods), certain that we will always love them, only for those same things to cause us to balk as older adults. In short, our goals change (and a lot more than we think they are going to). We enthusiastically marry people in our thirties whom we later divorce in our forties. We try several careers before we find the right fit. A potential antidote to this is to make our longer-term goals not only SMART, but also conscious.

TRY IT: SET MORE CONSCIOUS GOALS

It is easy to fall into the trap of setting what we might call *gullible goals*. The kind of goal we have simply inherited from the television ('You need a shinier kitchen'), or perhaps from the judgemental comments of the previous generation ('Why aren't you married yet?'). Conscious goals, on the other hand, take into account what we, as individuals, actually want and need. Look around at the world and you will notice that it is remarkably easy to have a shiny kitchen and a spouse and still be deeply unhappy. Next time you set a goal, make it conscious by considering these two questions:

1. *Where was this goal modelled to me?* If the answer is a glossy magazine or a dictatorial family elder, then you may like to think it through a bit further before committing. Be critical of the sources of your goals (and check that you aren't being falsely sold an ideal).

2. *What part of me yearns for this goal?* Do you want a relationship because the vulnerable part of yourself wants to feel accepted? Or a new kitchen to make the part that didn't have much in childhood feel prosperous? Once you put your finger on who within you wants this thing, it might be possible to put the desire in context, imagine alternatives or seek new paths to getting it that may well be less external or material, and more about doing some deeper self-reflection and inner work.

The Vision Board

A popular way to put one's goals onto paper is the vision board. This graphic depiction of our desires will be likely to include both words and pictures cut from magazines and newspapers, representing things we really want. Vision boards can be very meaningful, but they can also tend towards the materialistic. When our primary resource for this activity is mainstream media, we can end up having rather more pictures of shoes and holidays than the things that truly make us feel good: connection, rest and freedom to be who we are without embellishments. Thus, it might be a good idea to think not only about what our dreams might *look like* on a vision board, but also how we want them to *feel*.

You may think that what you want is a holiday home, but what if what you really want is quality time with your family – is there another way to get this? A wardrobe full of designer garb may appeal, but perhaps you just really want to feel respected and admired by others – if so, how else might this be achieved? This isn't to say that 'things' never bring their practical benefits, but just that, more often than not, it's the *feeling* and not the *stuff* for which we hunger. Try applying this idea to a vision board in the following way:

1. *Begin by collecting up any images that speak to you, without sticking them down yet.* Avoid overthinking at this stage – you do not have to use all the images, so just gather any that make you feel

a spark of interest, without analysis of why. Shoes and holidays are, of course, allowed, but ensure you are also gathering images that may speak to your less 'flashy' desires for friendship, warmth and easy contentment.

2. **Once you have collected your images, sort them into several piles, each centred on a visible theme.** For example, you might have lots of interior design pictures that will form one pile, and images of sandy beaches in another. Play with these piles until you are happy with them.

3. **Next, sit with each pile of images for a few moments.** Lay them out in front of you and think about how they make you feel. You might want to close your eyes, holding the images in your mind's eye, and notice any physical sensations they bring up for you: excitement and butterflies? Relief? A dropping of the shoulders?

4. **Then, take some colourful notepaper and write any feelings you associate with the pile.** You might write one big theme word or phrase in the centre, e.g. the sandy beaches might cause you to write 'calm' as your

theme word, with other associated words and feelings around this such as 'carefree', 'untethered' or 'totally relaxed'.

5. *Having done this for each pile, revisit the magazines for any images you may have missed that speak to a feeling rather than any particular thing.* Instead of clipping out more sandy beaches, find other things that make you feel calm that might be more imminently attainable: a cup of tea, a hot bath or time outdoors on local rural walks.

6. *Finally, it's time to start sticking!* Arrange your vision board however feels right, mixing in your new images with the original ones and incorporating your 'feeling words' in a way that works for you. This way, when you look to your vision board you will remember that it is not always things we want, sometimes it is a feeling we crave. It can be fun to strive for ambitious goals, but don't delay those positive feelings if you can also find them – however fleetingly – in your everyday life.

The Meal Plan

Each week, whatever happens and however work is going or family life is progressing, one truth remains constant: we will always need to eat. Yet this most basic necessity – that one would think we might all have come to terms with by now – can cause us all manner of stress. We make stressful midweek runs to the corner shop for a can of chopped tomatoes or an onion. We create mountains of washing up that nobody can face tackling at 9pm on a Wednesday. We waste leftovers and half-jars of pesto that we forgot were there and perhaps spend rather too much on takeaway food because we simply cannot deal with thinking up and preparing another meal from scratch. One way to quell this madness, that you may have tried, is the meal plan.

Whether you are meal-planning for one or getting a family of four's eating organized, the concept is simple enough: before the start of a new week, set out a menu of easy yet nutritious lunches and dinners that you plan to make over the coming days. This allows you to shop accordingly, as well as perhaps even do some batch cooking or chopping to prepare. You might use an app such as Weekly Chefs, set this out on a whiteboard hung in your kitchen, write it in your ordinary planner or on a large sheet of paper that you stick to the fridge. However you plan your meals, here are some tips for making this ritual more mindful:

TIPS FOR WRITING A MORE MINDFUL MEAL PLAN

Plan in colour. One of the simplest and most enjoyable ways to get a balanced diet is, simply, to eat a wide variety of fresh fruit and vegetables – and a good way to track this is to observe how much colour there is in your diet. Use coloured pens and pencils when you put together your meal plan, to get an at-a-glance visual of the variety in your diet (e.g. highlight your morning green smoothie in green). If you are struggling to think up new recipes or are stuck in a rut, try throwing in a 'purple' day when you base your lunch or dinner around that colour (aubergines, purple sprouting broccoli or red cabbage), or a 'yellow' day (yellow squash, yellow pepper or banana).

Plan for ease. Much of modern life is regimented. We might feel we have to act like impeccable robots to get by, and avoid being our more endearing-yet-flawed selves. For this reason, we can be tempted to be rather over-ambitious with our meal planning. Avoid expecting too much of yourself (life is hard enough) and, instead, plan for ease wherever possible; it is fine to schedule a takeaway night if your budget allows, as well as plan in leftover days when you don't have to cook. You can also include a mix of fresh, pre-prepared and frozen veg so that you get plenty of nutrients without too much onerous preparation.

Plan to talk. If you live and eat with others, one of the most satisfying elements of the sit-down meal is the conversation. Yet too often we sit scrolling on our phones, or bicker and gripe after a tense day. Counteract this by using your meal plan to set out not just what you will eat, but how you will enjoy eating it. Write down 'no phones' days, or agree a blanket rule on this. Make Mondays a chat about what everyone is looking forward to that week, or Fridays a review of good and bad things that happened. This way, a simple meal can be a way to build new family rituals that nourish connection as well as tummies.

The Timetable or Rota

When we are of school age it is typical that we get gifted a paper planner to set out our classes. As adults, when we want to plan a set of tasks out for multiple people – such as chores for a household – we turn to a rota. These ways of organizing our time help keep us on track and knowing where we should be, and what we should be doing when we get there.

Organizing others and ourselves in this way can be a daunting task and one that can become tense if not executed with care and compassion. Perhaps you are a freelancer bullying yourself with a weekly timetable to which you never seem to stick, or you are a parent desperate to organize help with dog-walking and dishes from your kids, but never seeming to get anywhere. What is important when we plan out the days and weeks of our lives is to allow for error. How might our timetables and rotas be changed for the better if we admitted to ourselves that we (and those we love) make rather a lot of errors, and can be quite rebellious? Perhaps we could then build in a little bit of friendly flexibility.

Any timetable or rota will benefit from falling somewhere between being too rigid (thus not allowing space for spontaneity, creativity and surprise) and too loose (becoming unstructured, disorganized and dauntingly messy). Take a look at yours and write down some notes in answer to these questions:

- **Where am I expecting too much?** e.g. working a full day on a Friday when you might finish a bit early, or setting your kids their chores as soon as they get in from school when they might benefit from a rest first.

- **Am I expecting too little?** e.g. are you leaving Sunday's completely un-timetabled where you might benefit from a scheduled hour of planning for the week to come?

- **Could I make this more fun?** e.g. leaving Monday mornings free from any meetings so that you can do some creative thinking, or 'gameifying' yours and your kids' chores with a sticker scoreboard.

- **Could I make this more efficient?** e.g. scheduling tricky tasks first thing (Google 'eat the frog' if you aren't familiar with this technique) and leaving low-stakes admin tasks for after lunch when you are typically tired and less focused.

Each question holds equal weight – a rota with no joy is an inherently inhumane and unsustainable one, and a timetable with no efficiency is pointless. Find your balance and take a chance to review these questions once per quarter or so, to check things feel on track.

Writing for Resilience

Resilience is the ability to weather the storms of life
– and we can all do it. All of us will have had
circumstances we felt we would never get through.
Nevertheless, here we are. *Through.* Yet how do we
continue to support ourselves when the storms just
keep on coming?

When bad things happen, it is not useful to simply think
positively. What *can be* useful, however, is to challenge
ourselves to be realistic about what
we can control and what we
cannot. To paraphrase the
ancient Stoic philosopher,
Epictetus, we must remember
that 'some things are up to us,
and others are not'.

There are many things that
we cannot, ultimately,

control: our environment, the current political climate, other people etc. Indeed, if you take the time to thoughtfully consider what you can control in any given situation, you might find that this sphere of influence is a lot smaller than you perhaps first thought. One of the few things we ever really control is *how we react to what happens*. That being said, your belief about an event markedly defines how you experience it. So, by critically engaging with how you think about a situation, you can make real change.

To build resilience then, it is important to put the groundwork in place so that when difficult situations arise, we can react in a more mindful and helpful way. One way to do this is known as the ABC model.

The 'ABC' Way to Write About Difficult Things

ABC stands for: **A**ctivating event, **B**eliefs about the event and **C**onsequence.[1]

The mistake that most of us make is to go directly from a difficult event (A), to the consequence (C), concluding that the two must be inextricably linked. What we miss is that *the consequence very often results from our belief,* not from the adversity itself. We neglect even the briefest analysis before we jump to the wrong conclusions.

For example, say you spot a colleague while out shopping; you call out but they ignore you (A) and you immediately feel distraught because, clearly, they do not actually like you (C). If you examine your belief you might ask: why is 'I am unlikeable' (B) the most realistic interpretation of this situation? In truth, there are many other beliefs you might have: that they simply didn't hear you, or that they had headphones in, or that they were having a bad day themselves and did not want you to see them upset...it could be anything. Our beliefs define so much about our experience, and they can be challenged.

Next time you need to bolster your resilience, try writing your own ABC followed by a short paragraph that challenges your belief. Ask what evidence is there for this belief? What if I am wrong about this?

Consider alternatives to the quick-fire interpretations you may have made. You may not instantly believe these alternatives – but this is a habit to practise over time: developing the capacity for healthier, more helpful ways of looking at what happens to you that will bolster your resolve.

Goals
and Plans
to Try

Whether or not we generally succeed with our goals,
the whole process can nevertheless become rather
exhausting. This is because, if we succeed, we tend to
focus our attention immediately upon the next big goal we
want. If we do not succeed, we beat ourselves up. In either
case we can become so caught up in self-flagellation –
i.e. berating ourselves that we never do enough or
complaining that we never do, well, *anything* – that we
simply become burnt out.

Finding a peaceful balance between being forward-
focused yet also enjoying the moment can be tricky to get
right. One way to tackle any hamster-wheel habits of

mindless goal-chasing might be to experiment with the *kinds* of goals we set. We can reflect thoughtfully upon the behaviours that govern us, the different outcomes we desire and the longer term rather than short-term vision we have for our life.

In his book *Happier*, teacher and positive psychology expert, Tal Ben-Shahar, reflects on winning the Israeli national squash championship when he was 16 – a major goal for which he had trained for the five preceding years. What followed was a period of low spirits as he looked around and thought 'What now?' He describes learning in the following years that, rather than a pinnacle we might one day reach, 'becoming happier is a lifelong pursuit'[4] – a journey with many highs, many setbacks and requiring a good deal of intentional practice.

Remember that your happiness, too, is a lifelong pursuit. Use the following, slightly unconventional ways to goal-set to help you prioritize peace and purpose on that journey, rather than foster a relentless obsession with success.

The Deliberate Daydream

We tend to think of self-discipline as essential to the fulfilment of goals. We envisage, perhaps, wrangling ourselves into submission – dragging ourselves to the gym or binding ourselves to our desk chair to write our novel. Yet, perhaps unsurprisingly, this rather aggressive conception of goal fulfilment might do more to make us feel miserable than productive. What if, instead, the enactment of our goals was something in which we took pleasure daily? What if goals were a way of, as the adage goes, living our dreams? Enter: daydreaming as a legitimate goal-setting technique.

Perhaps you were told off for daydreaming in your childhood: gazing in what appeared to be total absent-mindedness out of the window of your classroom before being snapped back to 'reality'. Yet the humble daydream may offer a helpful pathway to your most authentic goals.

The problem with a lot of goal-setting practices is that they do not take root in the self; they come from external sources like what we are told success looks like or social conventions we think we need to meet. Yet few things reflect the self better than the unbounded exploration of a daydream. In such a state we achieve a balance of conscious engagement (i.e. we are not asleep) as well as lessened intellectual intrusion (i.e. that critical inner voice is briefly switched off).

TRY IT: START A DELIBERATE DAYDREAMING PRACTICE

Daydreaming has been linked in many psychological studies to increased creativity – so much so that some researchers argue for 'deliberate daydreaming' as a way to boost our creative competency.[5] This is perhaps because the best goals require imagination – and imagination is not something we can predict and measure out in lists and graphs.

Typically, a daydream occurs spontaneously, but there are ways to initiate it. Studies in this area have utilized many methods for this, but here are three you might try alongside your writing. Set a timer for 20 minutes and go somewhere you will not be disturbed, then choose one as your focus.

A memory. Try to vividly recreate a happy memory in your mind. Picture what was happening and who was there. Hold this in your mind for a moment, and then allow it to 'prompt' any other images, beginning to let your mind wander freely.

An object. Think about an everyday object, picturing its qualities in your mind's eye. Then, mentally manipulate that object into another form, such as a ceramic bowl suddenly becoming liquid. Imagine several different forms before beginning to let your mind wander freely.

An imaginary trip. Think of a place, real or fictional, to which you would like to travel. Picture it in vivid detail. Spend some time mentally in this place, before beginning to let your mind wander freely.

Once you finish your deliberate daydream, write for a further five to ten minutes about what happened.

What might you learn from the daydream about the kind of person you are – about your hopes, ambitions and plans? This may not be immediately obvious, but over time this cultivation of creative thinking may just overhaul the way you look at your goals. Once we relinquish conscious control over our thoughts, as we do in a daydream where our mind wanders, we give ourselves permission to think differently – free from constraint and expectation.

The PURE Goal

Goals can make life worth living – but only if they are truly meaningful. If we pick the wrong goals there is every chance that they will fail to offer us any real satisfaction (and we may even feel worse as a result of pursuing them). Psychology researcher, Paul Wong, has proposed that there are four ingredients needed for truly meaningful life goals: Purpose, Understanding, Responsible Action, and Evaluation (or Enjoyment). Wong writes that this more meaningful model of goal-setting 'enables us to become aware of what we are striving for and thus avoid blindly pursuing things that will destroy us in the end'.[6] Next time you set a goal take the time to run it by these four principles, writing a brief response to each question.

1. *Purpose (i.e. our motivation)* Being purpose-driven offers us resilience and incentive to achieve our plans.
   Ask: What really matters to me in life – and in what ways does this particular goal reflect those core values?

2. **Understanding (i.e. our intellectual cognition)**
   Coherent understanding or making sense of
   ourselves and the world means our goals will likely
   be more realistic.
   Ask: what is my reasoning behind this goal? How
   does it mesh with the person I truly am and how the
   world truly is?

3. **Responsible Action (i.e. our behaviour)** Getting in
   touch with our moral sense of responsibility helps
   direct us in humane, kind and socially just directions.
   Ask: what is the right thing to do with the options
   available? What responsibility do I have in this
   situation?

4. **Evaluation (i.e. our emotions)** This is where we
   consider the question: am I enjoying myself?
   Ask: am I happy with how this goal makes me feel?
   (Note that if we find we are not happy, we might be
   prompted to begin the PURE cycle again.)

The Whim

Society can be rather negative about whims. We seem to classify acting out of impulse as really rather daft and are therefore used to ignoring our intuition. Goals and plans, we believe, require ample forethought, excessive written strategizing and many months of lead-time. The issue with ignoring one's whims is that we can end up doing rather more of what other people expect of us and rather less listening to ourselves.

When things go wrong and we turn to counsellors or therapists, one of the foremost things we are usually seeking is trust in ourselves to know what steps to take next. This makes sense; so much of what we consider 'maturity' seems to be about acquiescing to societal convention rather than flying the flag of our own – slightly zany or oddball – factory settings. If you feel you have been lacking trust in yourself, or ignoring your intuition for the sake of sticking to prescribed models for living, it may be time to develop deeper trust in yourself. Of course, to trust, we first have to *listen*.

TRY IT: WRITE DOWN YOUR WHIMS

Turn to a fresh page in your journal or a blank loose sheet of paper. Before you begin, close your eyes for a moment, taking a few slow deep breaths and putting both hands on your heart in acknowledgement of being present, quietly, with yourself. As you settle into a natural breath, say out loud or internally: 'I am listening'. It might feel right to repeat this a couple of times. If you sense that you have not always listened closely to yourself, and even ignored your inner voice for the sake of listening to louder, external voices, it might feel appropriate to say to yourself: 'I know I have not been listening, but I am now'. From here, begin writing from the following prompt:

When I really listen to myself, I hear that...

To be sure, acting on a whim will not always be the best course of action. Equally, ignoring our inner voice might mean years wasted on things we thought we 'should' do, but that we never really wanted. A written practice of listening to our whims – valuing them as equally as any more rigid or formal goal – is a good place to start striking this balance.

The Prayer

One traditional way that human beings have set goals is by praying for things to happen. Our typical image of this might be a person poised on their knees, perhaps at the foot of their bed, hands clasped as they appeal for world peace under their breath. What is interesting – and often really hard – in modern secular society is that we do not always believe we are getting any holy handouts to help us along with the tough stuff. Yet, does living as an atheist mean we must do away with prayer? Perhaps not.

In his book, *Religion for Atheists*, Alain de Botton makes a case for borrowing some of the rather helpful elements of the world's centuries-old religions – including prayer. He argues for the very necessary comfort we can derive from such practices, writing that, far from being self-deluding, this kind of ritual highlights 'vulnerability as a virtue', therefore correcting our 'habitual tendency to believe in a conclusive division between adult and childhood selves'[7].

The power of religious prayer is to console us that a 'Father' or 'Mother' is listening with tenderness to the struggling, hopeful, delicate part of our self that is asking for help. In secular psychotherapeutic practice, getting in touch with this vulnerable or 'little' part of the self is often referred to as inner child work – widely recognized as a powerful form of healing and self-development. So, whether you are religious or not, the format of traditional prayer may offer a helpful way of getting in touch with the part of you that needs help – whatever the goal.

What we can do, whether spiritual or less so, is examine the ways in which we might benefit from a process of 're-parenting' ourselves. This can counter a habit of, when writing down plans for our lives, falling into two broad ways of communication with our self: the stern parent or the wilful child. We can accidentally develop an internal narrative of authoritarian discipline, or naughty unruliness – and in either case there are negative outcomes: either we become overly self-critical, overly slack or swing between the two.

TRY IT: WRITE A PRAYER WITH YOUR INNER CHILD

The essence of much prayer is that we ask a deity or saint for their support – yet this is not the only way to express what we need. It is possible to transcend the self without necessarily visualizing and addressing a divine figure floating in the heavens. The comforting power of prayer may be, as Alain de Botton suggests, simply in acknowledging our neediness – and perhaps appealing to an 'inner parent': that part of us who is not stern, but kind and supportive. Try writing responses to the following:

The most vulnerable part of me is asking for.
The help I need is...
The vulnerability I see in others is...
The help they need is...

If you are spiritual you might direct these questions to the higher power in which you put your faith. If you are an atheist, simply acknowledge these needs and express hope that this clarity will aid your search for more material forms of support.

The Story

One often overlooked way that we plan out our lives is through stories. Once we grasp this we understand the influence of media on our lives. Movies can teach us unhelpful gender 'norms' like masculine hyper-strength, or more helpful qualities like being brave whatever our gender. Novels can model romantic love as the supreme goal for a woman's life, or teach us more balanced ways of living such as the importance of having many good friends.

An essential feature of any conscious goal-setting is to become closely aware of the input we receive around what kinds of goals we *should* have. Movies, literature and media more broadly all combine to show us what the world is like – to teach us, in other words, how to live. In fact, researchers argue that fictional narratives offer a simulation of real life[8]. Stories teach us how to be in the world and set out paths for us to follow. As psychologist and novelist, Keith Oatley, writes: 'Fiction is about possible selves in possible worlds' – in other words, stories are a way that we set (or, perhaps more precisely, *inherit*) goals.

TRY IT: EXPLORE YOUR STORIES

Have you ever stopped to think about how the stories you have been exposed to have directed – and continue to direct your life? Write a response to each of the below.

You might write this as a list, a narrative or a bit of both – whatever feels right. Note that 'stories' here is used in the broadest sense. You might think of literal storybooks, films, TV shows, plays, folklore and fairy tales, common analogies, advice from others, the news, and/or politics... Any 'plotlines' you have picked up from the world.

Stories that influenced me in my young life were...
Stories that influenced me as a teenager/young adult were...
Stories that are influencing me now are...

After reviewing these past stories, have a go at the following:

A new story I would like to write is one where...

Afterword: The Pleasure of Writing

Writing is a significant vehicle for personal change and, because of this, for social change. When we articulate ourselves to ourselves – in lists and notes and diaries – we understand ourselves better as a result. What is powerful about this is that, in knowing how we operate (i.e. making an honest appraisal of our flaws and triggers as well as our strengths and virtues) we are better equipped to empathize with how others operate. Another way we can describe this phenomenon is as emotional literacy – a mighty tool for connecting us together as groups and communities.

One important way in which we can become more emotionally literate is in noticing the distinction between *eudaimonic* and *hedonic* happiness – a distinction made by both classic philosophy and modern psychology alike. Eudaimonic happiness can be thought of as a deeply purposeful or noble happiness, which may not always be overtly pleasurable in the moment, but is deeply meaningful for us nonetheless (e.g. studying for a degree, or planting a garden). Hedonic happiness is the experience of positive, pleasurable feelings and sensations (e.g. enjoying a funny film, or eating some food we love).

Parenthood provides a useful illustration of this concept. While having children may temporarily, or even in the long term, reduce our experience of pleasurable feelings (hedonic happiness) due to broken sleep, stress and prioritizing the needs of a new little person over our own, ultimately, for most, parenthood has a deep-rooted significance (eudaimonic happiness). Whether parents or not, many of us will have experienced moments of wellbeing when eudaimonic and hedonic happiness occur simultaneously, such as the endorphins we feel from exercise (hedonically pleasurable) even though we are training for a charity run (eudaimonic). Upon reflection, we may even find we actively pursue more of these 'simultaneous' forms of happiness.

There are varying arguments around these two different versions of happiness. Some argue they exist entirely independently, some say that one can actively reduce the other, while others contend that they are not really all that different. We can leave those arguments to the researchers for now and instead ask: how might these two ideas of wellbeing work in my real life – and in my writing specifically?

Firstly, merely having an awareness of these two sides of the happiness coin is useful. It can help us be resilient through difficult times by providing the comforting notion that adverse immediate situations might well be contributing to our overall wellbeing in the long term. Secondly, this dual understanding of wellbeing helps us to prioritize our daily goals and pursuits. While staying in bed, eating biscuits and watching an entire season of our favourite TV show might fill us with gleefully pleasurable feeling now and again, we would be hard pressed to describe this as a meaningful pursuit in the long term.

Use your writing practices – whether note-taking, goal-setting or otherwise – to observe your daily experience of hedonic and eudaimonic wellness. In doing so, witness the balance you tend to strike between the two, maybe even viewing some of your favourite hedonic pleasures (a glass of wine with friends) as a reward for your more eudaimonic pursuits (study, work or exercise etc.)

Of course, the *activity* of writing is in itself both a hedonic and eudaimonic pleasure. There is the humble hedonic indulgence of quiet time to our self with good stationery and just our own thoughts for company; and there is also the eudaimonic sense of purpose and connection writing offers. We write for the joy of getting to know who we are, and also the (perhaps slightly trickier) joy of understanding *the world we live in*. We write ultimately for the opportunity to, now and again, positively impact both. It is in this spirit – both pleasurable and noble – that we find the true joy of writing things down.

ʻEnd Notes

INTRODUCTION

1 George A Kelly, *The Psychology of Personal Constructs*, vol. 1 (London: Routledge, 1991).

2 Natalie Goldberg, *Writing Down the Bones: Freeing the Writer Within*, (Boston: Shambhala Publications Inc., 2005).

3 Adeline van Waning, 'A Mindful Self and Beyond: Sharing in the Ongoing Dialogue of Buddhism and Psychoanalysis', in *Awakening and Insight: Zen Buddhism and Psychotherapy*, Polly Young-Eisendrath and Shoji Muramoto (London: Taylor & Francis Group, 2002): 91–102.

4 Definition is from the *Oxford Dictionary of English*.

5 Hubert J M Hermans, 'The Dialogical Self: A Process of Positioning in Space and Time', in *The Oxford Handbook of the Self*, ed. Shaun Gallagher (Oxford: Oxford University Press, 2013): 654–80.

6 Charles Fernyhough, *The Voices Within: The History and Science of How We Talk to Ourselves* (New York: Basic Books, 2016).

7 Carl R Rogers, *A Way of Being* (New York: Houghton Mifflin Harcourt, 1995): 114–17.

8 Y T Seih et al., 'The Benefits of Psychological Displacement in Diary Writing When Using Different Pronouns', *British Journal of Health Psychology* 13, no. 1 (2008): 39–41.

9 Megan Hayes, 'The Flourishing Writer', *Writing in Practice: The Journal of Creative Writing Research* 3 (2017).

10 Carl R Rogers, *On Becoming a Person* (London: Constable, 2004):122.

CHAPTER 1

1 Eva Von Contzen, 'The Limits of Narration: Lists and Literary History', *Style* 50, no. 3 (2016): 241–260.

2 E J Masicampo and Roy F Baumeister, 'Consider It Done! Plan Making Can Eliminate the Cognitive Effects of Unfulfilled Goals.', *Journal of Personality and Social Psychology* 101, no. 4 (2011): 667.

3 Michael K Scullin et al., 'The Effects of Bedtime Writing on Difficulty Falling Asleep: A Polysomnographic Study Comparing To-Do Lists and Completed Activity Lists', *Journal of Experimental Psychology*. General 147, no. 1 (January 2018): 139–46.

4 Carol D Ryff, 'Psychological Well-Being Revisited: Advances in the Science and Practice of Eudaimonia', *Psychotherapy and Psychosomatics* 83, no. 1 (2014): 10–28.

5 Laura A King, 'The Health Benefits of Writing about Life Goals', *Personality and Social Psychology Bulletin* 27, no. 7 (2001): 798–807.

6 David de Meza and Chris Dawson, 'Neither an Optimist Nor a Pessimist Be: Mistaken Expectations Lower Well-Being', *Personality and Social Psychology Bulletin*, 6 July 2020.

7 Lewis Hyde, 'The Gift Community', in *The Gift: How the Creative Spirit Transforms the World*, Main-Canons

imprint re-issue edition (Edinburgh: Canongate, 2007): 76–94.

8 C R Snyder, 'Hope Theory: Rainbows in the Mind', *Psychological Inquiry* 13, no. 4 (1 October 2002): 249–75.

9 Barbara L Fredrickson, 'Positive Emotions Broaden and Build', in *Advances in Experimental Social Psychology*, vol. 47 (Burlington: Academic Press, 2013): 1–53.

10 'Find Your 24 Character Strengths | Personal Strengths List | VIA Institute', accessed 24 July 2020.

11 Ryan M Niemiec, 'Six Functions of Character Strengths for Thriving at Times of Adversity and Opportunity: A Theoretical Perspective', *Applied Research in Quality of Life* 15, no. 2 (2020): 551–572.

12 Kennon M Sheldon, 'Becoming Oneself: The Central Role of Self-Concordant Goal Selection', *Personality and Social Psychology Review* 18, no. 4 (1 November 2014): 349–65.

13 Celia Hunt, *Therapeutic Dimensions of Autobiography in Creative Writing* (London: Jessica Kingsley Publishers, 2008): 33–35.

Feature Spread

1 Shauna L Shapiro, The integration of Mindfulness and Psychology. *Journal of Clinical Psychology* 65, no. 6 (2009): 555-560

CHAPTER 2

1 Nathaniel M Lambert et al., 'To Belong Is to Matter: Sense of Belonging Enhances Meaning in Life', *Personality and Social Psychology Bulletin* 39, no. 11 (1 November 2013): 1418–27.

2 Matthew Kelly, *The Seven Levels of Intimacy: The Art of Loving and the Joy of Being Loved* (New York: Fireside, 2007).

3 Gloria Mark et al., 'Email Duration, Batching and Self-Interruption: Patterns of Email Use on Productivity and Stress', in *Proceedings of the 2016 CHI Conference on Human Factors in Computing Systems*, 2016, 1717–1728.

4 Matthias R Mehl et al., 'Eavesdropping on Happiness: Well-Being Is Related to Having Less Small Talk and More Substantive Conversations', *Psychological Science* 21, no. 4 (1 April 2010): 539–41.

5 Amir Levine and Rachel Heller, *Attached: Are You Anxious, Avoidant or Secure? How the Science of Adult Attachment Can Help You Find – and Keep – Love* (London: Bluebird, 2019).

6 Pema Chödrön, *The Places That Scare You: A Guide to Fearlessness* (Element, 2001), 16–23.

7 Chödrön: 73–80.

8 Chödrön: 73–89.

9 'Gratitude Letter (Greater Good in Action)', accessed 1 September 2020.

10 Lilian J Shin et al., 'Gratitude in Collectivist and Individualist Cultures', *The Journal of Positive Psychology* 15, no. 5 (2020): 598–604.

Feature Spread

1 Roz Ivanič, *Writing and Identity: The Discoursal Construction of Identity in Academic Writing* (Amsterdam: John Benjamins Publishing, 1998), 16.

CHAPTER 3

1 Lev Semenovich Vygotsky, *Thought and Language*, trans. Eugenia Hanfmann, Gertrude Vakar and Alex Kozulin (Cambridge, Massachusetts: The MIT Press, 2012).

2 Pema Chödrön, *The Places That Scare You: A Guide to Fearlessness* (London: Element, 2001): 137–42.

3 Chödrön: 162.

4 '10 Steps to Savoring the Good Things in Life', Greater Good, accessed 7 September 2020.

5 David K Sherman, 'Self-Affirmation: Understanding the Effects', *Social and Personality Psychology Compass* 7, no. 11 (2013): 834.

6 David K Sherman and Kimberly A Hartson, 'Reconciling Self-Protection with Self-Improvement: Self-Affirmation Theory', in *Handbook of Self-Enhancement and Self-Protection*, ed. Mark D Alicke and Constantine Sedikides (New York: The Guilford Press, 2011):130.

7 Nils F Toepfer et al., 'Examining Explanatory Mechanisms of Positive and Expressive Writing: Towards a Resource-Oriented Perspective', *The Journal of Positive Psychology* 11, no. 2 (3 March 2016): 124–34.

8 Larry Chang, *Wisdom for the Soul: Five Millennia of Prescriptions for Spiritual Healing* (Washington D.C.: Gnosophia Publishers, 2006).

9 Y T Seih et al., 'The Benefits of Psychological Displacement in Diary Writing When Using Different Pronouns', *British Journal of Health Psychology* 13, no. 1 (2008): 39–41.

CHAPTER 4

1 Hubert J M Hermans, 'The Dialogical Self: Toward a Theory of Personal and Cultural Positioning', *Culture & Psychology* 7, no. 3 (2001): 249.

2 Hubert J M Hermans, 'Self as a Society of I-Positions: A Dialogical Approach to Counseling', *The Journal of Humanistic Counseling* 53, no. 2 (2014): 147.

3 Paul John Eakin, *Fictions in Autobiography: Studies in the Art of Self-Invention* (Princeton: Princeton University Press, 1985): 277.

4 Natalie Goldberg, *Writing Down the Bones: Freeing the Writer Within* (Boston: Shambhala Publications Inc, 2005).

5 Julia Cameron, *The Artist's Way: A Course in Discovering and Recovering Your Creative Self*, new edit/cover edition (London: Pan, 1995).

6 Peter Elbow, *Writing Without Teachers* (New York: Oxford University Press, 1998).

7 Gillie E J Bolton, *Reflective Practice: Writing and Professional Development*, third edition (London: SAGE Publications Ltd, 2010).

8 Peter A Caprariello and Harry T Reis, 'To Do, to Have, or to Share? Valuing Experiences over Material Possessions Depends on the Involvement of Others', *Journal of Personality and Social Psychology* 104, no. 2 (2013): 199–215.

9 Ryder Carroll, *The Bullet Journal Method: Track the Past, Order the Present, Design the Future* (London: Fourth Estate, 2018).

10 Tristine Rainer, *The New Diary: How to Use a Journal for Self-Guidance and Expanded Creativity* (New York: Tarcher/Penguin, 2004): 206.

11 Rainer: 156.

Feature Spread

Kristin Neff, 'Self-Compassion Journal', Self-Compassion (blog), 23 February 2015.

CHAPTER 5

1 Gordon B Moskowitz and Heidi Grant (eds), *The Psychology of Goals* (New York: Guilford Press, 2009): 1.

2 Richard M Ryan and Edward L Deci, 'Self-Determination Theory and the Facilitation of Intrinsic Motivation, Social Development, and Well-Being', *American Psychologist* 55, no. 1 (2000): 68.

3 Daniel Gilbert, *Stumbling on Happiness* (London: Harper Perennial, 2007).

4 Tal Ben-Shahar, *Happier: Can You Learn to Be Happy?* (New York: McGraw-Hill Education, 2008): 8.

5 Claire M Zedelius and Jonathan W Schooler, 'The Richness of Inner Experience: Relating Styles of Daydreaming to Creative Processes', *Frontiers in Psychology* 6 (2016).

6 Paul T P Wong, 'Toward a Dual-Systems Model of What Makes Life Worth Living', *The Human Quest for Meaning: Theories, Research, and Applications 2* (2012): 10.

7 Alain de Botton, *Religion for Atheists: A Non-Believer's Guide to the Uses of Religion* (London: Penguin UK, 2012): 175.

8 Raymond A Mar and Keith Oatley, 'The Function of Fiction Is the Abstraction and Simulation of Social Experience', *Perspectives on Psychological Science* 3, no. 3 (1 May 2008): 173–92.

Feature Spread

Barbara Teater, 'Cognitive Behavioural Therapy (CBT)', in *The Blackwell Companion to Social Work*, ed. Martin Davies (London: John Wiley & Sons, 2013): 423–27.

Further Reading

Gillie Bolton, *Write Yourself: Creative Writing and Personal Development* (London: Jessica Kingsley Publishers, 2011).

Celia Hunt, *Therapeutic Dimensions of Autobiography in Creative Writing* (London: Jessica Kingsley Publishers, 2008).

Greta Solomon, *Heart, Sass & Soul: Journal Your Way to Inspiration and Happiness* (Mango, 2019).

Ira Progoff, *At a Journal Workshop: Writing to Access the Power of the Unconscious and Evoke Creative Ability* (Jeremy P Tarcher, 1992).

Julia Cameron, *The Artist's Way: A Course in Discovering and Recovering Your Creative Self* (Pan, 1995).

Natalie Goldberg, *Writing Down the Bones: Freeing the Writer Within* (Boston: Shambhala Publications Inc, 2005).

Pema Chödrön, *The Places That Scare You: A Guide to Fearlessness* (Element, 2001).

Tristine Rainer, *The New Diary: How to Use a Journal for Self-Guidance and Expanded Creativity* (Tarcher/Penguin, 2004).

ALSO BY MEGAN

Write Yourself Happy
The Happiness Passport
The Serenity Passport

Index

'ABC' way to write about difficult things 182–3
address books 40–1
affirmations 43, 123–4
aphorisms 125–7
attachment styles 72–3
attention 11–13
autofiction 162–3

Ben-Shahar, Tal *Happier* 185
Berry, Wendell 'The Peace of Wild Things' 48
'best-possible self' 38–40
birthday books 40–1
Bolton, Gillie 141
bucket lists 38–40
Buddhism 78–9, 88, 92, 101, 105–6, 111–12, 128
Zen Buddhism 12, 14–15, 26
bullet journals 145–7

calm 114–17
Cameron, Julia *The Artist's Way* 140
cards 77–9
Caroll, Ryder 145–6
Chödrön, Pema 78
Collins, Billy 'Marginalia' 109

compassion 77–9, 153–5
confidence 82–5
congruence 17–18
correspondence 63–6
correspondence to try 86–97
correspondence you're already writing 67–8
emails 69–71
greetings cards or letters 77–9
instant messaging 71–3
postcards 79–81
social media posts 74–6
creativity 8–9
creative journals 161–3

daydreaming, deliberate 185–8
de Botton, Alain *Religion for Atheists* 192, 193
diaries see journals and diaries
donations 42–3
dreams 156–7

Eakin, Paul John 136
emails 69–71
tonglen email 92–3

emotions 143, 189
emotions lists 52–3
empathy 19–20
Epictetus 181

five senses lists 50–1
focus 46–8
Frankl, Victor *Man's Search for Meaning* 125–6
freewriting 139–41
Gilbert, Daniel *Stumbling on Happiness* 172

goals 165–8
goals to try 184–95
goals you're already writing 169–70
PURE goals 188–9
resolutions 170–2
setting more conscious goals 173
SMART goals 172
vision boards 174–6
gratitude 42
gratitude letters 94–5
savouring notes 121–3
greetings cards 77–9
groundlessness 111–12

happiness 197–9
Hermans, Hubert 132
Hunt, Celia 57–8, 59

ideas 107–8
in-between notes 128–9
inner dialogue 16–17, 19–20
  self-compassion 153–5
insights 108–9
instant messaging 71–3
integrative writing 151–2
internal censor audit 149–51
Ivanić, Rosalind 83

Jahoda, Marie 36
journals and diaries 131–3
  bullet journals 145–7
  daily diary 135–9
  dream diary 156–7
  freewriting 139–41
  journal and diary writing to try 148–9
  journal and diary writing you're already doing 134–5
  reflective journals 141–3
  travel journals 144–5
  what is it like to be you? 136–8

writing for self-compassion 153–5
Jung, Carl 36

letters 77–9, 87–9, 94–5
life lists (or 'life calendars') 57–61
lists 29–31, 49
  address or birthday lists 40–1
  bucket lists 38–40
  lists to try 49–61
  lists you're already writing 32–3
  project lists 43–5
  shopping lists 42–3
  to-do lists 34–7

maitri letters 87–9
Marcus Aurelius Meditations 119, 120
marginalia 109–10
meal plans 176–8
meaning 125–6
  developing a meaning mindset 126–7
meditations 119–21
morning messages 90–1
motivation 44–5, 171–2, 188

nature 48
Neff, Kristen 153–4
Neisser, Ulric 136
Neruda, Pablo Odes to Common Things 47

Newton, Isaac 109
notes to self 99–102
  ideas 107–8
  insights 108–9
  marginalia 109–10
  notes to try 118–29
  notes you're already writing 103–4
  observations 110–12
  quotations 112–13
  reminders 104–6

Oatley, Keith 194
observations 110–12
Oliver, Mary 135

pathway thinking 44–5
pen portraits 48
Pennebaker, James W 13
plans 165–8
  meal plans 176–8
  plans to try 184–95
  timetables or rotas 179–80
  vision boards 174–6
Plath, Sylvia 109
play 79–80
pleasure of writing 197–9
positivity 18–19, 21–3
  positive journals 158–60
postcards 79–81
prayers 192–3

write a prayer with your inner child 193–4
project lists 43–5
PURE goals 188–9

quotations 112–13

Rainer, Tristine *The New Diary* 151, 156
reflective journals 141–3
reminders 104–6
resilience 181–3
resolutions 170–2
Rogers, Carl 16, 23, 36
rotas 179–80
Ryff, Carol 36

savouring notes 121–3
self-compassion 153–5
self-knowledge 135–6
  Conceptual Self 138–9
  Ecological Self 136–7
  Extended Self 137–8
  Interpersonal Self 137
  Private Self 138
shopping lists 42–3
SMART goals 172
social media posts 74
  three tips to help

you balance your ego 74–6
Socrates 113
spaciousness 101
stories 38–40, 194
  explore your stories 194–5
strengths lists 54–5

ta da lists 56–7
task avoidance 105–6
therapeutic writing 12–13, 143
timetables 179–80
to-do lists 34
  categorizing your to-do list 36–7
  sharing your to-do list 34–5
  writing your to-do list at bedtime 35
to-not-do lists 56–7
travel journals 144–5
trust 115–16
  write yourself a trusting note 117

unconditional positive regard 18–19

vision boards 174
  assembling your vision board 174–6

wellbeing categories 37
whims 190
  write down your whims 191

whole person communication 96–7
Wilde, Oscar 109
Winnicott, Donald 80
Wong, Paul 126, 188
writing 6–9
  bringing it all together 24
  making your writing habits more helpful 16–20
  making your writing habits more joyful 21–3
  mindful writing 26–7
  philosophy of writing 9–12
  pleasure of writing 197–9
  rewards of writing 25
  therapeutic effects 12–13, 143
  writing for calm 114–17
  writing for confidence 82–5
  writing for focus 46–7
  writing for resilience 181–3
  writing for self-compassion 153–5
  Zen of writing 14–15

Yi Cheng Lin 20

Acknowledgements

I would like to express my warmest thanks to Philippa Wilkinson and Julia Shone; it is always a sincere pleasure to work with you both and I hope there will be more projects to come. My gratitude also goes to Romy Palstra and Tokiko Morishima for the simply lovely illustrations and design, and to the whole team at Greenfinch for working to bring this book to life. A special thanks is due, as always, to my fantastic agent, Jane Graham Maw, for your continued support and expert guidance. I would also like to thank Linda Finlay for your kindness and for being the teacher I needed in 2020 (a tough year to write a book or do, well, anything). My thanks also go to Tim Webster for nattering with me over coffee as the ideas in this book took shape (and for all those beans you ground that kept me caffeinated). Finally, I am forever grateful to my family and friends; your support means everything.